MEMORIES OF
CHRISTMAS
PAST

MEMORIES OF
CHRISTMAS
PAST

By Betsey Langford and Carolyn Nixon

MEMORIES OF CHRISTMAS PAST

By Betsey Langford and Carolyn Nixon

Editor: Kimber Mitchell
Designer: Kelly Ludwig
Photography: Aaron T. Leimkuehler
Illustration: Eric Sears
Technical Editor: Christina DeArmond
Production assistance: Jo Ann Groves

Published by:
Kansas City Star Books
1729 Grand Blvd.
Kansas City, Missouri, USA 64108

First edition, first printing
ISBN: 978-1-61169-038-5
Library of Congress Control Number: 2011944804
Printed in the United States of America
By Walsworth Publishing Co., Marceline, MO

❧ TABLE OF CONTENTS ❧

❧ ABOUT THE AUTHORS ❧

Betsey Langford (right) and *Carolyn Nixon* (left) share the quilting heritage of cardboard templates, hand piecing, hand quilting, and hand binding. However, their quilting journeys began along different paths and times.

From birth, Carolyn was surrounded by handmade quilts and their makings. A primitive quilting frame hung from the ceiling over her bed. Her earliest memories are filled with the clicking of needle against thimble and the rhythmic motion of her mother's hand, rocking back and forth as she stitched together quilt blocks.

Betsey started quilting at the age of 18. Her Grandma Mary told stories and traded Sunday afternoon hand piecing lessons for Betsey's willingness to rotary-cut quilt pieces. Grandma Mary's lessons were of the old-fashioned sort; everything from the cutting to the quilting was done by hand.

Betsey and Carolyn started designing patterns together while they were co-owners of Quilted Heart, a quilt shop in Bolivar, Missouri. *Memories of Christmas Past* is their first book with Kansas City Star Quilts.

❧ DEDICATION ❧

This book is dedicated to Carolyn's mother, Pearl Brown, and Betsey's grandmother, Mary Cross. Our fond memories of them are ever-present companions in our lives. As young girls, we never knew how much those cardboard templates, scraps of fabric, needles, and thimbles would mean in our lifetimes. Thank you, Mama and Grandma Mary, for being strong women with a passion for creating, sharing, and passing on the legacy of quilting.

❧ ACKNOWLEDGMENTS ❧

OUR HEARTFELT APPRECIATION GOES TO:

* Diane McLendon and Doug Weaver of Kansas City Star Books for allowing us to fulfill our dream of sharing our quilt and projects with quilters around the world.

* Our editor, Kimber Mitchell, who has provided support, advice, and encouragement throughout this wonderful adventure.

* Our designer, Kelly Ludwig, for capturing the heart of our work in her design.

* Our illustrator, Eric Sears, for creating the perfect illustrations.

* Our technical editor, Christina DeArmond, for checking the accuracy of our instructions.

* Production assistant, Jo Ann Groves, for using her amazing eye for color and accuracy to create picture-perfect photos.

* Edie McGinnis and our photographer, Aaron Leimkuehler, who made the photo shoot a fun-filled day of learning and laughter.

* Thanks especially to Betsey's aunt and uncle, Lynn and John Rockeman, for welcoming us into their beautiful home for our location photo shoot and for giving us free rein over it to stage shots for our feature quilt and companion projects.

* Our sewing companions, Nancy Jones, Liz Kerr, Susie Geurin, and Becky Marsolf. Your positive and encouraging spirits are always a blessing.

A special thanks to Liz for the quick turnaround in quilting the Super Star Throw.

* Jerri Smith for her faithful assistance during our time at our former quilt shop, Quilted Heart.

* Our wonderful families. Your support and tolerance of our relentless sewing pursuits is a constant source of comfort. From the bottom of our hearts and the tips of our toes, we love and thank you, Donna, Laura, Whitney, Greg, Emily, Sara, and the "mixed family."

❧ INTRODUCTION ❧

*O*ur *Memories of Christmas Past* quilt began as a limited edition block-of-the-week project from our former quilt shop, Quilted Heart, in Bolivar, Missouri. Some might consider the notion of doing a block-of-the-week quilt rather daring. Even we wondered if our customers would seriously entertain the idea! It all started in the fall of 2008, when we made plans for a holiday shop promotion called the "Twelve Weeks of Christmas." The idea was to create a series of small projects that would make relatively quick and inexpensive gifts.

As our conversation unfolded, we decided to expand our promotion with a larger quilting project based on a series of journals about Carolyn's life growing up in the Ozarks. Since both of us love Nine-Patch blocks, we decided to design 12 sampler blocks using traditional block designs while spicing them up with a Nine-Patch twist. The entire project literally evolved week by week throughout the fall of 2008. The final design featured a stunning central medallion of Nine-Patch blocks and paper-pieced Poinsettia blocks.

With a block-of-the week project, we did not know what kind of reaction to expect from our customers. We were pleasantly surprised to find the response was unbelievable! In less than two weeks, we cut and sold 30 kits for our holiday quilt. Its success sparked another conversation about how we could share our quilt with a larger audience of quilters. And the rest of the story? Well, you are holding it in your hands!

Each of the blocks in the feature quilt is accompanied by a nostalgic entry from Carolyn's journals, recalling her childhood memories. In addition to the feature quilt, we have also created a series of companion projects that make great gift ideas—a memories journal, a framed quilt block, a throw pillow, a star-studded table runner, a quick and easy quilted throw, and a snowflake embroidery design. If you don't want to tackle a larger quilt, these smaller projects are the perfect alternative. And with that, we welcome you to *Memories of Christmas Past*.

Enjoy!

Carolyn Betsy

❧ Precision Quiltmaking Tips ❧

*W*hen *Carolyn* started teaching quilt classes at her former quilt shop, one thing quickly became evident. Most of the problems her students encountered were the result of imprecise cutting, piecing, and pressing. To help solve their dilemmas, she taught them these important quilting lessons, which she calls the "Three Ps of Quilting." Here are her tips for precision cutting, piecing, and pressing.

Cut precisely

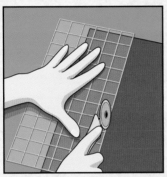

* Use the same type of ruler throughout the cutting process.
* If you are using templates, follow the pattern template exactly.

Stitch precisely

* Butt fabric edges together carefully.
* Sew a perfect ¼" seam by using a ¼" foot on your sewing machine.
* Avoid shifting your fabric sideways at the beginning and end of each seam. To help guide the fabric while stitching, Carolyn uses a sewing stiletto.

Press precisely

* Finger-press seams.
* Use an up-and-down pressing motion rather than a back-and-forth one.

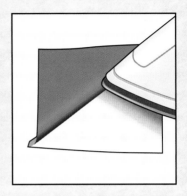

* To help stabilize the blocks and prevent fraying, Carolyn likes to use Best Press or Magic Sizing.

Betsey's Super Pressing Tip

Did you know a piece of tempered glass works great for precision pressing? Ask your local glass dealer for a ¼"-thick piece of tempered glass. After pressing your units, position them under the tempered glass until they cool. Your seams will be nice and flat, resulting in a more precise block.

MEMORIES OF CHRISTMAS PAST

MEMORIES OF CHRISTMAS PAST

MACHINE PIECED BY BETSEY LANGFORD AND CAROLYN NIXON

MACHINE QUILTED BY BARBARA STEPHENS

FINISHED QUILT SIZE: 86" X 86"

FABRIC REQUIREMENTS

QUILT BLOCKS, SETTING SQUARES, SETTING TRIANGLES, AND CORNER TRIANGLES:

* 4½ yards cream print
* ⅓ yard light red tone-on-tone
* ⅓ yard dark red tone-on-tone
* ⅓ yard white polka dot
* ¼ yard white print
* ¼ yard white/green print
* ½ yard brown print
* ⅓ yard green print
* ⅓ yard red polka dot
* ⅓ yard red paisley
* ⅓ yard red/green stripe
* ¼ yard green polka dot
* ¼ yard tan print
* ¼ yard green paisley
* ⅛ yard brown polka dot
* ⅛ yard white paisley

BLOCK FRAMES, OUTER BORDER, AND RED NINE-PATCH UNITS:

* 3½ yards red tone-on-tone
* Cream print yardage listed at left under the first listing

INNER BORDER, POINSETTIA BLOCKS, AND GREEN NINE-PATCH UNITS:

* 1⅔ yards green tone-on-tone
* Cream print yardage listed at left under the first listing

BINDING:

* ⅔ yard red print

BACKING:

* 8¼ yards fabric of your choice

The following memory of my parents, Charlie and Pearl Brown, is etched in my mind. It is my first vivid memory of growing up in Oregon County, Missouri, in the late 1950s.

A small girl sits perched on the edge of an old, wooden chair, her head bent intently over a book. The soft flicker of light from a kerosene lamp is the only defense against the darkness of an autumn night in the Ozark Hill Country. Across the room is the girl's father. Exhausted from the backbreaking labor of another long day working in the woods, his face is drawn and worn-looking.

Carolyn Nixon as a first grader at Rover Elementary School, 1958-59

Besides the repeated turning of the pages of the little girl's book, the only other sound comes from the industrious movements of a third person in the room. She sits in an oak rocking chair near the table, her brows knitted intently over the project in her hands. Despite the dim light, she works diligently to join oddly-shaped pieces of colored remnants cut from discarded clothing. The steady, metallic clicking of needle against thimble echoes in the night, marking the passing of evening and the creation of another quilt.

Suddenly, the silence of the September night is broken by a faint honking sound from somewhere overhead in the night sky. The girl's eyes move from the book to glance out the living room window toward Rover, Missouri, to the east. "What's that sound, Daddy?" she asks.

Drawing a deep breath, the man replies, "That's geese flyin' south, honey. Winter's a comin'. They'll come back this way again in the spring."

The woman in the chair does not respond at all. She hears nothing—not the sound from the night sky, the question, or the reply. She just sews.

My mother couldn't hear. At the age of eight, she endured a high temperature from rheumatic fever, which left her almost totally deaf in both ears. Fortunately for me, the hearing loss did not affect her creative spirit.

FOR BLOCK BACKGROUND, CUT:

* ✳ 4—4¼" x 4¼" squares from cream print

FOR NINE-PATCH UNITS, CUT:

* ✳ 2—1¾" strips the width of fabric from brown print
* ✳ 1—1¾" x 10" strip from brown print
* ✳ 1—1¾" strip the width of fabric from white/green print
* ✳ 2—1¾" x 10" strips from white/green print

SEWING INSTRUCTIONS

1. Sew a 1¾" x width of fabric brown print strip to each side of a 1¾" x width of fabric white/green print strip. Press the seams toward the brown print strips. Then cut the unit into 10—1¾"-wide segments.

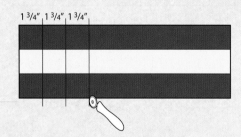

2. Sew a 1¾" x 10" white/green print strip to each side of a 1¾" x 10" brown print strip. Press the seams toward the brown print strip. Then cut the unit into five 1¾"-wide segments.

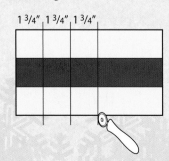

3. Sew together the three rows from steps 1 and 2 to create a Nine-Patch unit, which should measure 4¼" square unfinished. Press the seams toward the top and bottom rows. Repeat to create a total of five Nine-Patch units.

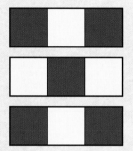

4. Referring to the following block assembly diagram, sew together the five Nine-Patch units and four 4¼" cream print squares to complete the block. The block should measure 11¾" square unfinished.

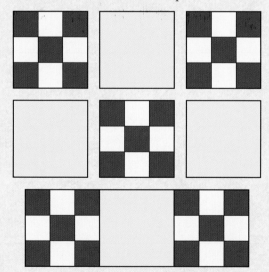

Block Assembly Diagram

Carolyn and her brother, Royce Brown, outside the County Line Store in 1952

When the before-dawn October air is thick with something between summer dew and autumn frost, my mind often travels back to childhood days. Funny how the seasons of our lives are marked by such vivid memories.

Daddy is always eager to start a new day, especially if there is money to be made. No matter how hard the weekdays are, October Saturdays are not made for sleeping, and "burnin' daylight" is not an option at our house.

My family is poor, at least as far as money is concerned. We have to make do with whatever resources are available to us. A woodsman by trade, my father knows the lay of the land for miles around our little four-room country house. This gives us an advantage over the neighbors in locating the walnut groves. Because Daddy is on good terms with all the landowners, we have their permission to gather up loads of Ozark black gold—green-hulled nuggets full of tasty kernels.

On weekends I am required to join the walnut pick-up crew. I never know where we will end up on these October days, but several things are sure: my young back will be aching at nightfall, my fingers and hands will be stained a dirty brown color that resists even the strongest of lye soap, and we will keep at it until there are no more walnuts to throw into burlap tow sacks—or the buyer stops buying.

At the end of each workday, we haul those sacks of walnuts to West Plains for hulling and weighing. The reward is real money, and Daddy always gives me a bit of my own to spend. Often, the money never makes it all the way back home with me. If we stop at the Thompson's County Line store for gas or groceries, I am only too happy to hand over the funds to the proprietor in exchange for something cold and delicious to eat or drink.

18

FOR BLOCK BACKGROUND, CUT:

* 3—3" x 3" squares from white polka dot. Then cut squares twice diagonally from corner to corner, yielding 12 triangles
* 2—3¾" x 3¾" squares from white polka dot
* 1—2¼" x 4½" rectangle from white polka dot
* 2—2¼" x 2¼" squares from white polka dot

FOR CARPENTER'S WHEEL, CUT:

* 8—2⅛" x 2⅛" squares from green print
* 4—1¾" x 3¼" rectangles from green print
* 4—1¾" x 4½" rectangles from green print

FOR NINE-PATCH UNIT, CUT:

* 2—2¼" x 4½" rectangles from red paisley
* 1—2¼" x 2¼" square from red paisley

FOR OUTER CORNERS, CUT:

* 2—4½" x 4½" squares from red/green stripe. Then cut square once diagonally from corner to corner, yielding four triangles

SEWING INSTRUCTIONS

1. Sew a 2¼" x 4½" red paisley rectangle to each side of a 2¼" x 4½" white polka dot rectangle. Press the seams toward the red paisley rectangles. Referring to the following diagram, cut the resulting unit in half, creating two rows.

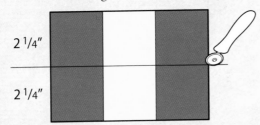

2¼"

2¼"

2. Sew a 2¼" white polka dot square to each side of a 2¼" red paisley square. Press the seams toward the red paisley square.

3. Sew together the three rows from steps 1 and 2 to create a Nine-Patch unit, which should measure 5¾" square unfinished. Press the seams toward the top and bottom rows.

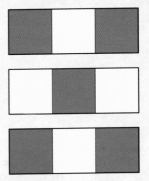

4. Referring to the following diagram, sew a white polka dot triangle cut from a 3" square to a 1¾" x 3¼" green print rectangle. Press the seam toward the green print rectangle. Make a total of four of these units.

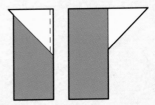

5. Referring to the following diagram for placement, sew a 1¾" x 4½" green print rectangle to the unit from step 4. Press the seam toward the triangle unit.

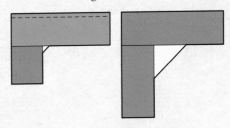

6. Trim the corners off the rectangles, using the bottom of the white polka dot triangle as a guide. Make a total of four of these units.

7. Sew a triangle unit to each side of the Nine-Patch unit. Press the seams toward the outer triangle units. The resulting unit should measure 7⅞" square unfinished.

8. Draw a diagonal line once from corner to corner on the wrong side of the 2⅛" green print squares.

9. With right sides together, layer two marked 2⅛" green print squares on opposite diagonal corners of a 3¾" white polka dot square. Sew a ¼" seam on both sides of the line, then cut apart on the drawn line. Press the seams toward the green print triangles.

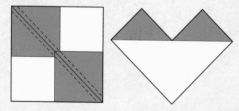

10. With right sides together, layer a marked 2⅛" green print square on the corner of the unit created in the previous step. Sew a ¼" seam on both sides of the line. Then cut apart on the drawn line. Press the seams toward the white polka dot triangle to create a Flying Geese unit. Trim the Flying Geese unit to measure 1¾" x 3" unfinished.

11. Repeat steps 9 and 10 to create a total of eight Flying Geese units.

12. Sew together two Flying Geese units. Then sew a white polka dot triangle cut from the 3" squares to each end of the two Flying Geese units. Press the seams toward the white polka dot triangles. Repeat to make a total of four of these units.

13. Sew a red/green stripe triangle cut from the 4½" squares to the top of each unit created in step 12. Press the seam toward the red/green stripe triangle. Repeat to make a total of four of these units.

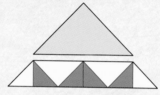

14. Referring to the following block assembly diagram, sew the four Flying Geese units from step 13 to the four corners of the Nine-Patch unit. Press the seams toward the Nine-Patch unit. The block should measure 11¾" square unfinished.

BLOCK ASSEMBLY DIAGRAM

I close my eyes and struggle through decades of fog to fold back a wrinkle in time. The journey back through time seems long and troublesome today, but eventually it leads to a cool, October morning and a sleeping child.

I sleep safely, my tightly-curled body surrounded by the warmth of feathers captured within a covering of thick, blue-striped ticking. Beneath my head is a feather pillow. Resting across me are layers of quilts. The top one is a hand-tied collage of color and textures. As I wake and stretch in the cool October Sunday morning, strands of knotted, red crochet thread tickle my nose. Above me is Mama's quilting frame, corners twisted up and held close to the bedroom ceiling by bailing twine; it is the same frame she used when she systematically punched and pulled a darning needle strung with red thread to tie the quilt covering me.

"Get up, Sissy," says Mama. "You better eat some breakfast. We gotta haul wood today." Begrudgingly, I drag myself from the warmth of the bed, get dressed, and go to the kitchen. After a breakfast of biscuits and gravy, we head out in Daddy's old log truck. I know it will be a long day full of hard work. There is no way to avoid any of it. Winter is coming, and the only way to stay warm is to have wood to feed the hungry stoves that wage battle against cold winds in a house constructed with no insulation.

Throughout the day, Daddy, Mama, and I travel to the timber to collect the wood that Daddy has already spent days laboring to cut for us. We toss the winter fuel onto the back of the truck and drive back home to unload and stack it. Four times the pattern is repeated. Lunch, a meal of cold fried chicken, bread buns, and fried apple pies, is somewhere in between.

Hours later, the fruit of our labor is clearly visible. Firewood is stacked neatly in three-deep, five-foot-high rows on each side of our front porch. Another huge heap is piled on the west side of the porch, waiting to be carted up as the rows on the porch disappear throughout the cold months ahead.

Carolyn with nephews David and Danny Walker
after a day of hauling and stacking wood

CUTTING INSTRUCTIONS

FOR BLOCK BACKGROUND, CUT:

✳ 2—4⅝" x 4⅝" squares from cream print

✳ 4—4¼" x 4¼" squares from cream print

FOR STAR POINTS, CUT:

✳ 2—4⅝" x 4⅝" squares from red paisley

FOR NINE-PATCH UNIT, CUT:

✳ 2—1¾" x 3½" rectangles from green polka dot

✳ 1—1¾" x 1¾" square from green polka dot

✳ 1—1¾" x 3½" rectangle from tan print

✳ 2—1¾" x 1¾" squares from tan print

SEWING INSTRUCTIONS

1. Sew a 1¾" x 3½" green polka dot rectangle to each side of a 1¾" x 3½" tan print rectangle. Press the seams toward the tan print rectangle. Referring to the following diagram, cut the resulting unit in half, creating two rows.

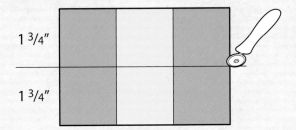

2. Sew a 1¾" tan print square to each side of a 1¾" green polka dot square. Press the seams toward the green polka dot square.

3. Sew together the three rows from steps 1 and 2 to create a Nine-Patch unit, which should measure 4¼" square unfinished. Press the seams toward the top and bottom rows.

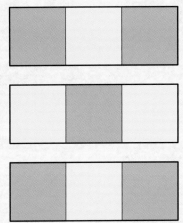

4. Draw a diagonal line once from corner to corner on the wrong side of both 4⅝" cream print squares.

5. With right sides together, layer a marked 4⅝" cream print square on top of a 4⅝" red paisley square. Sew a ¼" seam on both sides of the line, then cut apart on the drawn line. Press the seam toward the red paisley triangle. Trim the half-square triangle units to measure 4¼" square unfinished. Repeat this step for the other cream print and red paisley squares to make a total of four half-square triangle units.

6. Referring to the following block assembly diagram, sew together the Nine-Patch unit, the four half-square triangle units from the previous step, and the four 4¼" cream print squares to complete the block. The block should measure 11¾" square unfinished.

BLOCK ASSEMBLY DIAGRAM

Autumn has declared possession of the Ozarks. Fencerows and roadsides are ablaze with the splendor of red sumac. Walnut trees are all but naked, and other varieties are clinging tenaciously to their dying cloaks of leaves. Forest pathways are strewn with carpets of brown and burnished gold. It all reminds me so much of childhood days 50 years past. As I struggle to find my way back home, I am sure of only one thing—love really is homemade.

Carolyn's mother, Pearl Brown, on her wedding day

With fall butchering done and hundreds of cans of vegetables lining the cellar wall, Mama starts to settle in for the winter by cutting out quilt pieces. Times are hard, and money for fabric is an unaffordable luxury, so she works at recycling whatever clothes have reached the end of their usefulness as wearing apparel. Daddy's old shirts and any other worn pieces of clothing that she can find became prime targets for her scrutiny and the razor-sharp blades of her scissors. Nothing is wasted. If there are buttons, zippers, lace, hooks, and eyes, well, Mama saves them all. After snipping off all the recyclable parts, she works meticulously to salvage every scrap possible from around the holes and worn-thin fabric of the elbows, knees, and collars.

GOOD BOYS & GIRLS

CUTTING INSTRUCTIONS

FOR BLOCK BACKGROUND, CUT:
* 4—2⅛" x 2⅛" squares from cream print
* 4—1¾" x 5½" rectangles from cream print
* 8—2½" x 2½" squares from cream print

FOR PAW POINTS, CUT:
* 8—2½" x 2½" squares from white/green print

FOR CENTER SQUARE, CUT:
* 1—1¾" x 1¾" square from white/green print

FOR NINE-PATCH UNITS, CUT:
* 2—1⅝" x 15" strips from red polka dot
* 1—1⅝" x 7" strip from red polka dot
* 2—1⅝" x 7" strips from white print
* 1—1⅝" x 15" strip from white print

SEWING INSTRUCTIONS

1. Sew a 1⅝" x 15" red polka dot strip to each side of a 1⅝" x 15" white print strip. Press the seams toward the red polka dot strips, then cut the unit into eight 1⅝"-wide segments.

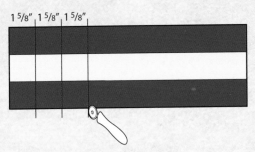

2. Sew a 1⅝" x 7" white print strip to each side of a 1⅝" x 7" red polka dot strip. Press the seams toward the red polka dot strip, then cut the unit into four 1⅝"-wide segments.

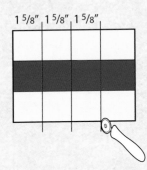

3. Sew together the three rows from steps 1 and 2 to create a Nine-Patch unit, which should measure 3⅞" square unfinished. Press the seams toward the top and bottom rows. Repeat this step to make a total of four Nine-Patch units.

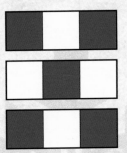

4. Draw a diagonal line once from corner to corner on the wrong side of the 2½" cream print squares.

5. With right sides together, layer a marked 2½" cream print square on top of a 2½" white/green print square. Sew a ¼" seam on both sides of the line, then cut apart on the drawn line. Press the seam toward the white/green print. Trim the half-square triangle units to 2⅛" square unfinished. Repeat this step for the other cream print and white/green print squares to make a total of 16 half-square triangle units.

6. Sew four half-square triangle units from step 5 into two different sets as shown below. Please note that one is the reverse of the other. Then make a total of four of each of the sets. Press the seams toward the cream print triangles.

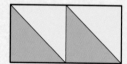 

7. Sew a 2⅛" cream print square to the end of four of the half-square triangle units, reversing two of them. Press the seam toward the cream print square.

 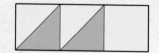

8. Referring to the following diagram, sew a unit from step 6 to a Nine-Patch unit and repeat to make a second unit. Press the seams to the Nine-Patch units.

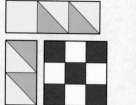 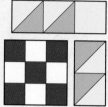

9. Referring to the previous diagram, sew a unit from step 7 to the top of each of the units from step 8. Press the seams toward the Nine-Patch units. Each unit should measure 5½" square unfinished. Repeat to make a total of four of these units.

10. Referring to the following block assembly diagram, sew the four units from step 9, the four 1¾" x 5½" cream print rectangles, and a 1¾" white/green square to complete the block. The block should measure 11¾" square unfinished.

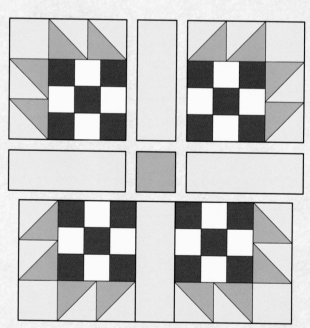

BLOCK ASSEMBLY DIAGRAM

Life in the country was filled with critters—fat ones, furry ones, feathered ones, creepy-crawly ones, ones that howled and kept us up at night, and ones that woke us up in the morning—the list goes on and on!

October evenings are lengthening, and the sun has long gone down before the swaying light of Daddy's lantern marks our advance to the barnyard where the cows stand waiting for feed and milking. The chill in the air is accentuated by a fine mist of cold rain.

"Daddy, can I sit on old Bossy tonight?" I ask.

"I guess," he replies as he pats one of the cows on the hindquarters, urging her into the barn first. "Let me get her in the stanchion first. Then I'll give you a boost up."

Daddy lifts me up to sit astraddle my favorite critter, a mild-mannered Jersey cow. As usual, old Bossy doesn't even bat her big, soft cow eyelashes; she just starts chewing blissfully away on the grain in her feed trough. She is quite accustomed to eating with me sitting on her back while Daddy milks her.

Ping! Squish! Slish! SHHHUSH! SHHHUSH! Daddy's hands patiently nurse the warm milk from Bossy's udder. The flow is sparse at first, but the stream of white grows steadily into sudsy rivers gushing against the side of the old metal bucket gripped between Daddy's knees as he sits perched on the edge of his grey, wooden milk bench.

A flurry of activity in the corner catches my attention. The sound and smell of warm, fresh milk always attracts a hoard of cats. "Here come the kitties, Daddy. They're hungry," I say.

"Those dang cats are always hungry," Daddy says. "Guess I'll have to feed 'em before we go back up to the house, honey."

And Daddy always did feed "those dang cats" before we traipsed back up to the house, carrying our own supply of rich, buttery cow's milk.

CUTTING INSTRUCTIONS

FOR BLOCK BACKGROUND, CUT:

* 1—5½" x 5½" square from cream print. Then cut square once diagonally from corner to corner, yielding two triangles. You will use only one triangle
* 2—2⅜" x 9" rectangles from cream print
* 1—4⅝" x 4⅝" square from cream print. Then cut square once diagonally from corner to corner, yielding two triangles. You will use only one triangle
* 2—Template As on page 34 from cream print (cut one reverse)
* 1—Template B from cream print

FOR BASKET, CUT:

* 2—Template Cs on page 34 from red paisley (cut one reverse)
* 1—Template D on page 34 from red paisley
* 1—2¾" x 2¾" square from red paisley. Then cut square once diagonally from corner to corner, yielding two triangles
* 2—1⅞" x 3¾" rectangles from red polka dot
* 1—1⅞" x 1⅞" square from red polka dot
* 1—1⅞" x 3¾" rectangle from red/green stripe
* 2—1⅞" x 1⅞" squares from red/green stripe
* 1—3¾" x 3¾" square from green print. Then cut square once diagonally from corner to corner, yielding two triangles. You will use only one triangle
* 1—7⅛" x 7⅛" square from green print. Then cut square twice diagonally from corner to corner, yielding four triangles. You will only use two of the triangles

SEWING INSTRUCTIONS

1. Sew a 1⅞" x 3¾" red polka dot rectangle to each side of a 1⅞" x 3¾" red/green stripe rectangle. Press the seams toward the red polka dot rectangles. Referring to the following diagram, cut the resulting unit in half, creating two rows.

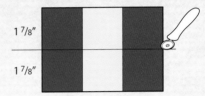

2. Sew a 1⅞" red/green stripe square to each side of a 1⅞" red paisley square. Press the seams toward the red paisley square.

3. Sew together the three rows from steps 1 and 2 to create a Nine-Patch unit, which should measure 4⅝" square unfinished. Press the seams toward the top and bottom rows.

4. Sew a green print triangle cut from the 7⅛" square to each side of the Nine-Patch unit. Press the seams toward the green print triangles.

5. Sew a green print triangle cut from the 3¾" square to the bottom of the Nine-Patch unit. Press the seam toward the green print triangle.

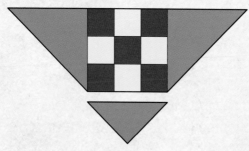

6. Referring to the top strip below, sew a red paisley triangle cut from the 2¾" square to a 2⅜" x 9" cream print rectangle to create a basket feet unit. Press the seam toward the red paisley triangle. Referring to the bottom strip below, repeat this step to create a second basket feet unit, reversing the triangle for the other side.

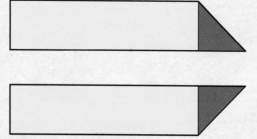

7. Referring to the block assembly diagram on page 33, sew the two basket feet units from the previous step to the sides of the basket. Press the seams toward the basket feet units. Trim the corners off the cream print rectangles, using the bottom of the green print triangle as a guide.

8. Referring to the block assembly diagram, sew a cream print triangle cut from the 4⅝" square to the base of the basket. Press the seam toward the cream print triangle.

9. To create the center handle unit, sew a red paisley Template D to a cream print Template B. Press the seam toward the red paisley unit.

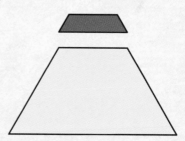

10. Referring to the first segment in the following diagram, sew a red paisley Template C to a cream print Template A to create a side handle unit. Press the seam toward the red paisley unit. Referring to the second segment in the following diagram, repeat this step to create a second side handle unit, reversing the placement of the templates.

11. Referring to the block assembly diagram, sew a side handle unit to each side of the center handle unit. Press the seams toward the side handle units.

12. Referring to the block assembly diagram, sew a cream print triangle cut from the 5½" square to the top of the handle unit. Press the seam toward the cream print.

13. Sew the handle unit to the rest of the basket block. Press the seam toward the handle unit. The block should measure 11¾" square unfinished.

BLOCK ASSEMBLY DIAGRAM

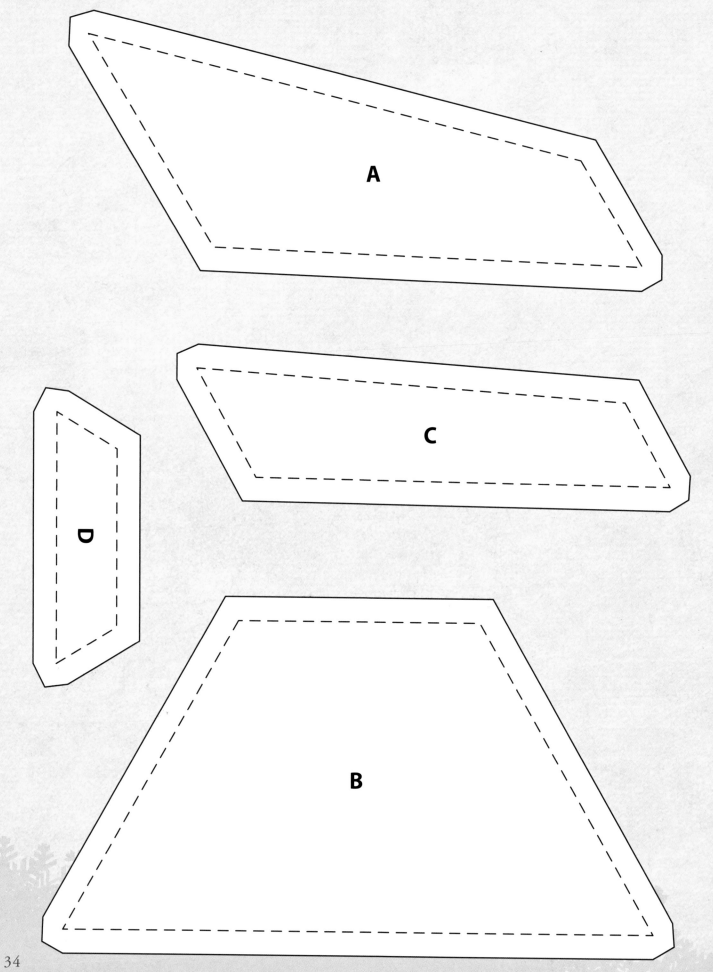

A

C

D

B

M ama loved Old Bossy's rich, buttery milk as much as the hoard of cats that lapped it up every evening in the barn. Unfortunately, her passion for the milk meant work for me. At least once a week, my job was to make butter. If Mama was really in a cooking mood, I had to do it two times a week. Making butter with a normal churn would have been one thing, but the way we did it was quite another. Our churn wasn't fancy; it was just an old gallon jar with a lid on it. Like most childhood adventures, the first time Mama allowed me to make butter, I felt like a big shot. Needless to say, my skinny, little arms tired easily, and that big-shot feeling fizzled like a lit match in a thunderstorm. I can still vaguely remember Mama telling me…

"It's nice outside today. Come on. Let's get you fixed up here on the back steps. Sit down, and I'll put the jar in your lap. You'll have to shake it like the dickens for the butter to separate, Carolyn Sue."

The rickety screen door slams shut behind us. I sit down on one of the steps, and Mama hands me the old gallon jar filled with cream. I start to shake it back and forth, from side to side. Shake. Shake. Shake. It isn't long before the novelty wears off, and my arms begin to feel like they are going to fall off. I rest a little while and then start shaking again. Shake a while, rest a while. Shake a while, rest a while.

After what seems like an eternity of shaking, there is a subtle change in the sloshing noises inside the jar. Peering into the jar, I see creamy clumps of butter and the buttermilk that Mama will use to make biscuits the next morning. I smile in relief.

In retrospect, I can truly say that the best part of making homemade butter was eating it on those homemade biscuits. What a scrumptious delight!

CUTTING INSTRUCTIONS

FOR LOG-CABIN UNIT, CUT:

* ✳ 1—2⅜" x 11¾" rectangle from brown print
* ✳ 1—2⅜" x 9⅞" rectangle from white paisley
* ✳ 1—2⅜" x 9⅞" rectangle from white polka dot
* ✳ 1—2⅜" x 8" rectangle from brown polka dot
* ✳ 1—2⅜" x 8" rectangle from red paisley
* ✳ 1—2⅜" x 6⅛" rectangle from white print
* ✳ 1—2⅜" x 6⅛" rectangle from white/green print
* ✳ 1—2⅜" x 4¼" rectangle from green print

FOR NINE-PATCH UNIT, CUT:

* ✳ 2—1¾" x 3½" rectangles from red polka dot
* ✳ 1—1¾" x 1¾" square from red polka dot
* ✳ 1—1¾" x 3½" rectangle from green paisley
* ✳ 2—1¾" x 1¾" squares from green paisley

SEWING INSTRUCTIONS

1. Sew a 1¾" x 3½" red polka dot rectangle to each side of a 1¾" x 3½" green paisley rectangle. Press the seams toward the red polka dot rectangles. Referring to the following diagram, cut the resulting unit in half, creating two rows.

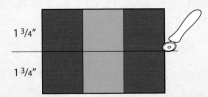

1 ¾"

1 ¾"

2. Sew a 1¾" green paisley square to each side of a 1¾" red polka dot square. Press the seams toward the red polka dot square.

3. Sew together the rows from steps 1 and 2 to create a Nine-Patch unit, which should measure 4¼" square unfinished. Press the seams toward the top and bottom rows.

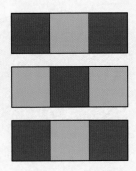

4. Referring to the following block assembly diagram, sew the 2⅜" x 4¼" green print rectangle to the Nine-Patch unit. Following the order of the numbers noted in the diagram, continue adding progressively longer rectangles to each side. With the addition of each rectangle, press the seams toward the one just added. The block should measure 11¾" square unfinished.

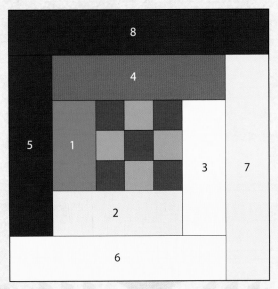

BLOCK ASSEMBLY DIAGRAM

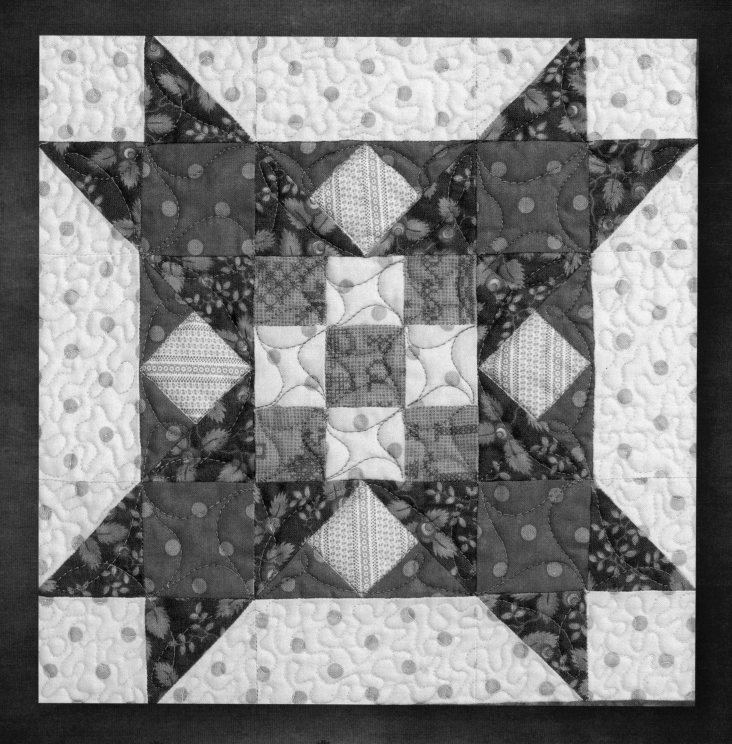

There is no memory as sweet as the vision of my mother's soft hands stitching on a quilt. Closing my eyes, I can remember her hands always working. I can see the split fingernail of her left forefinger and remember her telling the story of how it was injured by an old Singer sewing machine needle. Reaching across time and space, I can see Mama standing at the kitchen table…

Mama is wearing a handmade print dress. Skirting her waist is a worn calico apron. In the center of the table is a huge white well of flour. Mama mixes other ingredients in a bowl and then pours the mixture into the center of the flour. I watch in fascination as her hands work swiftly from side to side around the center of the well, folding the flour into the warm, yeasty mixture in the middle. Gradually, the dough forms into a soft ball, and the room fills with a familiar yeasty smell.

When the ball of dough feels just right under the touch of Mama's hands, she pauses to sift flour onto another bare spot on the table. She picks up the dough carefully and places it in the center of the sifted flour circle. Her skillful hands begin the task of kneading the bread dough to just the right consistency for rising.

When Mama turns to grease the large stoneware crock, I can resist no longer. It's just too tempting! My little fingers dart across the table to pinch away a bite of the dough and pop it into my mouth. Mama turns back to the table just in time to catch me in the act. "Don't be eatin' that bread dough, Carolyn Sue," she scolds me. "It'll make you sick."

"But, Mama, it hasn't ever made me sick yet," I say.

"Stop sassin' me, and keep your hands off that dough," she replies. "There'll be plenty for you to eat once it's baked, Sissy."

It makes me sad to think that this way of life is almost gone today— that many of America's children never sleep softly at night beneath a quilt made with loving hands or feast on homemade bread.

CUTTING INSTRUCTIONS

FOR BLOCK BACKGROUND, CUT:

* ❋ 1—1¾" x 3½" rectangle from white polka dot
* ❋ 2—1¾" x 1¾" squares from white polka dot
* ❋ 4—2⅜" x 2⅜" squares from white polka dot
* ❋ 4—2¾" x 2¾" squares from white polka dot
* ❋ 4—2⅜" x 4¼" rectangles from white polka dot

FOR STAR POINTS, CUT:

* ❋ 4—2¾" x 2¾" squares from brown print
* ❋ 4—2¾" x 2¾" squares from brown print. Then cut squares once diagonally from corner to corner, yielding two triangles

FOR CENTER FRAME, CUT:

* ❋ 4—2⅜" x 2⅜" squares from red polka dot
* ❋ 2—3⅛" x 3⅛" squares from red polka dot. Then cut squares twice diagonally from corner to corner, yielding eight triangles
* ❋ 4—1⅞" x 1⅞" squares from red/green stripe

FOR NINE-PATCH UNIT, CUT:

* ❋ 2—1¾ x 3½" rectangles from green print
* ❋ 1—1¾" x 1¾" square from green print

SEWING INSTRUCTIONS

1. Sew a 1¾" x 3½" green print rectangle to each side of a 1¾" x 3½" white polka dot rectangle. Press the seams toward the green print rectangles. Referring to the following diagram, cut the resulting unit in half, creating two rows.

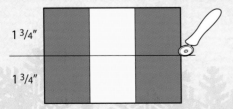

1 ³/4"

1 ³/4"

2. Sew a 1¾" white polka dot square to each side of a 1¾" green print square. Press the seams toward the green print square.

3. Sew together the three rows from steps 1 and 2 to create a Nine-Patch unit, which should measure 4¼" square unfinished. Press the seams toward the top and bottom rows.

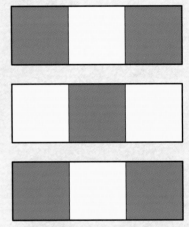

4. Sew a red polka dot triangle cut from the 3⅛" square to two adjacent sides of a 1⅞" red/green stripe square. Press the seams toward the red polka dot triangles. Repeat to make a total of four of these units.

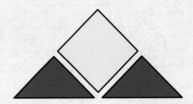

5. Sew a brown print triangle cut from the 2¾" square to two adjacent sides of the star point unit from the previous step. Press the seams toward the brown print triangles. The unit should measure 2⅜" x 4¼" unfinished. Repeat to make a total of four of these units.

6. Draw a diagonal line once from corner to corner on the wrong side of the 2¾" white polka dot squares.

7. With right sides together, layer a marked 2¾" white polka dot square on top of a 2¾" brown print square. Sew a ¼" seam on both sides of the line, then cut apart on the drawn line. Press the seam toward the brown print triangle. Trim the half-square triangle unit to 2⅜" square unfinished. Repeat this step for the other white polka dot and brown print squares to make a total of eight half-square triangle units.

8. Referring to the following block assembly diagram, sew together the Nine-Patch unit, the eight half-square triangle units from step 7, the four units from step 5, the four 2⅜" white polka dot squares, the four 2⅜" red polka dot squares, and the four 2⅜" x 4¼" white polka dot rectangles to complete the block. The block should measure 11¾" square unfinished.

BLOCK ASSEMBLY DIAGRAM

PATCH SQUARED BLOCK

It often feels like life rushes past me at lightning speed. My Google calendar is filled with meetings, conferences, training sessions, appointments, and my daughter's volleyball games. Days begin and end, and another pops up to start the cycle all over again. Interspersed are moments of sanity when I stop and dive deeply into the swirling waters of life to experience the sheer ecstasy of existence in this time and place. In such moments of quiet reflection, I realize that life doesn't rush past me; I am rushing past life. I'm reminded of that when I hear these words from the song "Mayberry" by Rascal Flatts: "Sometimes it feels like this world is spinning faster than it did in the old days, and we can't slow down 'cause more is best. It's all an endless process." I question whether more is best. There was a day when I had much less. I relive it from beginning to end, realizing how good it was.

Carolyn's parents, Charlie and Pearl Brown, in their front yard in Rover, Missouri, 1959

Before my eyes, Mama mixes cornmeal, water, salt, and a bit of sugar together into a lumpy batter. When it is just the right consistency, she gently molds it into the shape of an igloo, arranges it in the middle of a plate, and places it on a shelf in the old Frigidaire to chill. "We'll be havin' fried cornmeal mush tonight, Sissy," she says. "We'll have to make do til your Daddy gets paid on Saturday. Then we'll go down to Koshkonong and buy us a big turkey for Thanksgiving dinner."

Much later that evening, Daddy's face is drawn with fatigue. He sits in his easy chair, trying to recoup from another long day of hard work in the woods. Mama and I are again in the kitchen. I watch as she takes the cornmeal igloo out of the Frigidaire, slices it into half-inch chunks, and places it into an iron skillet to sizzle in hot grease. Sitting on the back of the iron cookstove is another pan filled with homemade syrup concocted from sugar and water. Supper is a warm, crispy fried cornmeal mush drizzled with butter and thin, sugary syrup. It is simple, meager, and real.

FOR BLOCK BACKGROUND, CUT:

* 2—6⅜" x 6⅜" squares from cream print. Then cut squares once diagonally from corner to corner, yielding two triangles

FOR FOUR CORNERS OUTSIDE OF NINE-PATCH, CUT:

* 2—5" x 5" squares from red/green stripe. Then cut each square once diagonally from corner to corner, yielding a total of four triangles

FOR NINE-PATCH UNIT, CUT:

* 2—2⅜" x 4¾" rectangles from red polka dot
* 1—2⅜" x 2⅜" square from red polka dot
* 1—2⅜" x 4¾" rectangle from white print
* 2—2⅜" x 2⅜" squares from white print

SEWING INSTRUCTIONS

1. Sew a 2⅜" x 4¾" red polka dot rectangle to each side of a 2⅜" x 4¾" white print rectangle. Press the seams toward the red polka dot rectangles. Referring to the following diagram, cut the resulting unit in half, creating two rows.

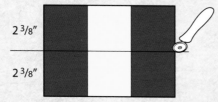

2 3/8"

2 3/8"

2. Sew a 2⅜" white print square to each side of a 2⅜" red polka dot square. Press the seams toward the red polka dot square.

3. Sew together the three rows from steps 1 and 2 to create a Nine-Patch unit, which should measure 6⅛" square unfinished. Press the seams toward the top and bottom rows.

4. Sew a red/green stripe triangle cut from the 5" squares to each side of the Nine-Patch unit. The resulting unit should measure 8¼" square unfinished. Press the seams toward the red/green stripe triangles.

5. Referring to the following block assembly diagram, sew a 6⅜" cream print triangle to each side of the unit from step 4. Press the seams toward the cream print triangles. The block should measure 11½" square unfinished.

BLOCK ASSEMBLY DIAGRAM

Thanksgiving and Christmas were always special days at our house. No matter how lean the times, Daddy somehow managed to have enough money for Mama to buy the makings of a feast for our family. Looking back, it seems that my mother was always happiest when she knew that her children and grandchildren would be coming to share a meal she had prepared.

It was quite the undertaking to cook for the 12-17 family members who showed up for holiday meals. The day before each of these holidays, Mama spent all day in the kitchen baking. What sweet memories—the smell of apple, cherry, and pumpkin pie; cinnamon rolls; and homemade buns. Although weary after a long day of laboring over a wood cookstove, Mama was always in a good mood the night before our gathering.

I remember her sitting on the divan playing silly games and asking me to recite the nursery rhymes that she had spent hours teaching me.

"You live up here," Mama says as she touches my forehead. "I live down here," she says, touching my chin. With a flick of her finger, she flips from my forehead down to my chin, smashing my nose in the process. "I come down to see you," she laughs.

"Chicken," she says, touching my forehead. "Rooster," she says, touching my chin. "Pullet," she says, touching my nose. "What did I say this was?" she asks, touching my nose again.

"Pullet," I reply.

"Okay," she says as she tweaks the end of my nose between her thumb and forefinger. "You said to pull it." No matter how many times she does it, I always say, "Pullet." Mama always responds by pulling my nose. We laugh, and then we laugh some more.

"Do Mama's Little Darlin', Sissy," Mama says to me. I oblige by placing my hands on my shoulders and responding with glee and animated gesturing. "Roses on my shoulders, slippers on my feet, I'm Mama's little darlin'. Don't you think I'm sweet?" Mama claps exuberantly and gives me a hug.

Carolyn wearing a flour sack
dress made by her mother

CUTTING INSTRUCTIONS

FOR BLOCK BACKGROUND, CUT:

* ✳ 4—3⅜" x 3⅜" squares from cream print
* ✳ 1—7" x 7" square from cream print

FOR STAR POINTS, CUT:

* ✳ 4—3¾" x 3¾" squares from brown print

FOR NINE-PATCH UNITS, CUT:

* ✳ 2—2⅜" x 4¾" rectangles from red polka dot
* ✳ 1—2⅜" x 2⅜" square from red polka dot
* ✳ 1—2⅜" x 4¾" rectangle from white/green print
* ✳ 2—2⅜" x 2⅜" squares from white/green print

SEWING INSTRUCTIONS

1. Sew a 2⅜" x 4¾" red polka dot rectangle to each side of a 2⅜" x 4¾" white/green print rectangle. Press the seams toward the red polka dot rectangles. Referring to the following diagram, cut the resulting unit in half, creating two rows.

2³/8"

2³/8"

2. Sew a 2⅜" white/green print square to each side of a 2⅜" red polka dot square. Press the seams toward the red polka dot square.

3. Sew together the three rows from steps 1 and 2 to create a Nine-Patch unit, which should measure 6⅛" square unfinished. Press the seams toward the top and bottom rows.

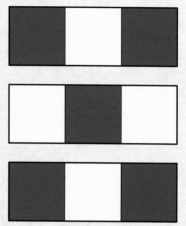

4. Draw a diagonal line once from corner to corner on the wrong side of the 3¾" brown print squares.

5. With right sides together, layer two marked 3¾" brown print squares on opposite corners of a 7" cream print square. Sew a ¼" seam on both sides of the line, then cut apart on the drawn line. Press the seams toward the brown print triangles.

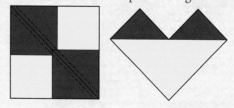

48

6. With right sides together, layer a marked 3¾"
   brown print square on the corner of the unit created
   in the previous step. Sew a ¼" seam on both sides
   of the line, then cut apart on the drawn line. Press
   the seams toward the brown print triangles to create
   a Flying Geese unit. Trim the Flying Geese unit to
   measure 3⅜" x 6⅛" unfinished. Repeat this step to
   create a total of four Flying Geese units.

7. Referring to the following block assembly diagram,
   sew together the Nine-Patch unit, the four Flying
   Geese units, and the four 3⅜" cream print squares
   to complete the block. This block should measure
   11⅞" unfinished.

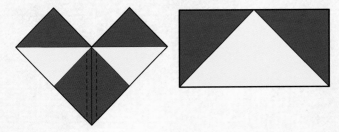

BLOCK ASSEMBLY DIAGRAM

Jack Frost still comes to paint ice sketches on windowpanes, just like he did when I was a child growing up in Oregon County, Missouri. These early December mornings of 2008 are not so very different from those of 40 or 50 years ago.

A soft, white blanket of snow covers the ground and flakes cascade from the grey, winter sky. The day is not good for Daddy to work in the woods, but it is good for cutting down a Christmas tree. This is one of the few rituals just for Daddy and me.

As always, we drive up and down gravel roads around our home, looking for just the right cedar tree. Red clay never stops cedars from growing in abundance. However, not just any tree will do for decorating. Daddy drives slowly, and several times we stop to check out a promising-looking specimen. Close scrutiny finds each tree lacking in some respect—too short, too fat, or too skinny.

Finally, about two miles east of our house, Daddy pulls to the edge of the road and lets the engine of the old log truck die. "Let's get out and walk a bit, Sissy. We can surely find a tree in this bunch," he says, motioning to a large grove of cedars beside the road. Snowflakes swirl gently around us as we make our way through the trees. Daddy is right. We find the perfect cedar tree in that little grove. I stand watching in delight as Daddy chops it down with his ax. We drag it back to the truck, and my father loads it on the bed of the truck.

Back at home, I am so excited to see the tree finally standing in the living room. Now, we can start putting decorations on it. Mama carefully unwraps my favorite ornament, a plastic star studded with brightly-colored bulbs that blink merrily from our front window every December. She hands the star to me, and Daddy lifts me up to place it on the topmost branch of the tree. The wonderful scent of cedar fills the small room, and I know that Christmas is just around the corner.

CUTTING INSTRUCTIONS

FOR BLOCK BACKGROUND, CUT:

* 4—4¼" x 2⅜" rectangles from tan print
* 6—2¾" x 2¾" squares from tan print

FOR CORNER UNITS, CUT:

* 2—2¾" x 2¾" squares from brown polka dot
* 4—2¾" x 2¾" squares from brown print. Then cut squares once diagonally from corner to corner, yielding eight triangles
* 2—4⅝" x 4⅝" squares from green polka dot. Then cut squares once diagonally from corner to corner, yielding four triangles

FOR FLYING GEESE UNITS, CUT:

* 1—5" x 5" square from green paisley

FOR NINE-PATCH UNIT, CUT:

* 2—1¾" x 3½" rectangles from red paisley
* 1—1¾" x 1¾" square from red paisley
* 1—1¾" x 3½" rectangle from white polka dot
* 2—1¾" x 1¾" squares from white polka dot

SEWING INSTRUCTIONS

1. Sew a 1¾" x 3½" red paisley rectangle to each side of a 1¾" x 3½" white polka dot rectangle. Press the seams toward the red paisley rectangles. Referring to the following diagram, cut the resulting unit in half, creating two rows.

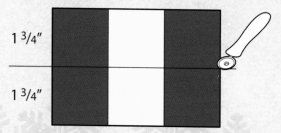

2. Sew a 1¾" white polka dot square to each side of a 1¾" red paisley square. Press the seams toward the red paisley square.

3. Sew together the three rows from steps 1 and 2 to create a Nine-Patch unit, which should measure 4¼" square unfinished. Press the seams toward the top and bottom rows.

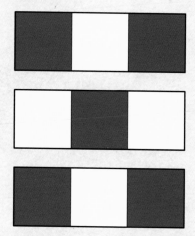

4. Draw a diagonal line once from corner to corner on the wrong side of two of the 2¾" tan print squares.

5. With right sides together, layer a marked 2¾" tan print square on top of a 2¾" brown polka dot square. Sew a ¼" seam on both sides of the line, then cut apart on the drawn line. Press the seam toward the brown polka dot triangle. Trim the half-square triangle units to 2⅜" square unfinished. Repeat this step for the other tan print and brown polka dot squares to make a total of four half-square triangle units.

6. Sew a brown print triangle cut from the 2¾" square to two adjacent sides of a half-square triangle unit. Press the seams toward the brown print. Repeat to make a total of four of these units.

7. Sew a green polka dot triangle cut from the 4⅝" square to the top of the unit from step 6. The finished unit should measure 4¼" square unfinished. Press the seam toward the green polka dot triangle. Repeat to make a total of four of these units.

8. Draw a diagonal line once from corner to corner on the wrong side of the 2¾" tan print squares.

9. With right sides together, layer two marked 2¾" tan print squares on opposite diagonal corners of a 5" green paisley square. Sew a ¼" seam on both sides of the line, then cut apart on the drawn line. Press the seams toward the tan print triangles.

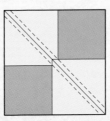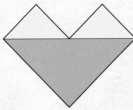

10. With right sides together, layer a marked 2¾" tan print square on the corner of the unit created in the previous step. Sew a ¼" seam on both sides of the line, then cut apart on the drawn line. Press the seams toward the tan print triangles to create a Flying Geese unit. Trim the Flying Geese unit to measure 2⅜ x 4¼" unfinished. Repeat this step to create a total of four Flying Geese units.

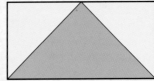

11. Sew a Flying Geese unit from the previous step to the top of a 2⅜" x 4¼" tan print rectangle. Repeat to create a total of four of these units.

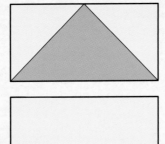

12. Referring to the following block assembly diagram, sew together the Nine-Patch unit, the four units from step 11, and the four units from step 6 to complete the block. Press the seams toward the units from step 11. The block should measure 11¾" square unfinished.

BLOCK ASSEMBLY DIAGRAM

CHURN PATCH BLOCK

I remember Ozark winters were hard. The world became shades of black, white, and gray. Maple and walnut trees in our yard stood naked against the onslaught of Mother Nature. Ragged winds rattled and squirmed through cracks in our house's thin windowpanes. The only truly warm places were the living room and the kitchen where we could stand or sit within range of one of the wood stoves. In the dead of winter, it was a daunting task just to keep the stoves fed with firewood.

Winter was also a magical time for me. I loved waking to a world of swirling snowflakes or a blanket of already-fallen snow. That was usually a clue that the big, yellow school bus would not be coming down the road to stop at my house. The day would be mine to do as I pleased, which usually meant reading a book or writing a story.

Carolyn and her parents, Charlie and Pearl Brown

All that reading and writing paid extra dividends on winter days of true adventure. Sometimes I was drawn outdoors by the prospect of swordplay. Any day when icicles were dangling from our roof was particularly promising for swordplay. Sometimes those icicles were two or three feet long. It was great fun to whack one down and grasp it in my hand as an age-old weapon like King Arthur. My imagination ran wild as I galloped through the snow on a broomstick steed, wielding my trusty sword at elusive fire-breathing dragons.

I have so much to thank my parents for, simple things like warmth, books to read, a yard to run and play in, cedar-tree Christmases, a world devoid of material things, a place to grow and become. Thanks, Mom and Dad. I love you.

FOR BLOCK BACKGROUND, CUT:

❋ 2—4⅝" x 4⅝" squares from cream print

❋ 1—2⅜" x 19" strip from cream print

FOR CHURN DASH, CUT:

❋ 2—4⅝" x 4⅝" squares from green paisley

❋ 1—2⅜" x 19" strip from green paisley

FOR NINE-PATCH UNIT, CUT:

❋ 2—1¾" x 3½" rectangles from brown print

❋ 1—1¾" x 1¾" square from brown print

❋ 1—1¾" x 3½" rectangle from white polka dot

❋ 2—1¾" x 1¾" squares from white polka dot

SEWING INSTRUCTIONS

1. Sew a 1¾" x 3½" brown print rectangle to each side of a 1¾" x 3½" white polka dot rectangle. Press the seams toward the brown print rectangles. Referring to the following diagram, cut the resulting unit in half, creating two rows.

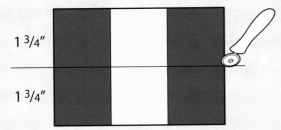

2. Sew a 1¾" white polka dot square to each side of a 1¾" brown print square. Press the seams toward the brown print square.

3. Sew together the three rows from steps 1 and 2 to create a Nine-Patch unit, which should measure 4¼" square unfinished. Press the seams toward the top and bottom rows.

4. Draw a diagonal line once from corner to corner on the wrong side of both 4⅝" cream print squares.

5. With right sides together, layer a marked 4⅝" cream print square on top of a 4⅝" green paisley square. Sew a ¼" seam on both sides of the line, then cut apart on the drawn line. Press the seam toward the green paisley triangle. Trim the half-square triangle units to measure 4" square unfinished. Repeat this step for the other cream print and green paisley squares to make a total of four half-square triangle units.

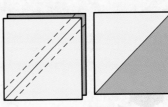

6. Sew a 2⅜" x 19" cream print strip to a 2⅜" x 19" green paisley strip. Press the seam toward the green paisley strip. Then cut the strip into four 4¼"-wide segments.

4 1/4"   4 1/4"   4 1/4"   4 1/4"

8. Referring to the following block assembly diagram,
    sew together the Nine-Patch unit, the four units
    from the previous step, and the four half-square
    triangle units from step 5 to complete the Churn
    Dash block. The block should measure 11¾" square
    unfinished.

7. The segments from step 6 will look like this when
    cut.

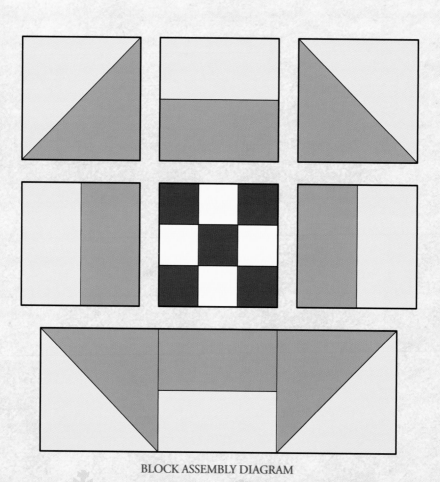

BLOCK ASSEMBLY DIAGRAM

58

OHIO PATCH BLOCK

A *blank piece* of paper reminds me that my nostalgic journey of the last three months is coming to a close. Part of me is incredibly sad to know that this is the final journal entry in the *Memories of Christmas Past* series. Another part of me smiles and is thankful for the rewarding experience of reflecting and writing about my childhood memories, about those I loved and those who loved me in return.

I'm looking forward to hugs and laughter this Christmas Eve when children and grandchildren gather in my house. Our family tradition harkens back to those set by my parents. Candles and oil lamps will light the house. Children will open packages, discarding paper and bows on the floor. They will giggle and perhaps have a spat or two before the evening ends. All will be well, and we can be thankful for another year of life and blessings.

Carolyn's mother and father, Pearl and Charlie Brown, on their 40th wedding anniversary

I originally thought this writing journey would end with a description of my favorite Christmas memory, a beautiful dollhouse with tiny pieces of elegant furniture and plastic people. But that seems inconsequential now. It seems more important to remind you all of how very precious and fleeting life is, to urge you to make the most of every minute of every day, to treasure your heart, your health, your loved ones, and all the blessings of your life, and to discover the best that is within you and pass it along to the next generation.

Fold it away
In the palm of their hearts
To be held gently
And quietly within.
Bask in the warm thought
Of being treasured
By someone who will still love you
In the distant tomorrow.

—Carolyn Brown Nixon

CUTTING INSTRUCTIONS

FOR BLOCK BACKGROUND, CUT:

▼ 4—4¼" x 4¼" squares from cream print

▼ 2—5" x 5" squares from cream print

FOR STAR POINTS, CUT:

▼ 2—5" x 5" squares from red paisley

FOR NINE-PATCH UNIT, CUT:

▼ 2—1¾" x 3½" rectangles from red/green stripe

▼ 1—1¾" x 1¾" square from red/green stripe

▼ 1—1¾" x 3½" rectangle from white polka dot

▼ 2—1¾" x 1¾" squares from white polka dot

SEWING INSTRUCTIONS

1. Sew a 1¾" x 3½" red/green stripe rectangle to each side of a 1¾" x 3½" white polka dot rectangle. Press the seams toward the red/green stripe print rectangles. Referring to the following diagram, cut the resulting unit in half, creating two rows.

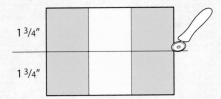

2. Sew a 1¾" white polka dot square to each side of a 1¾" red/green stripe square. Press the seams to the red/green stripe square.

3. Sew together the three rows from steps 1 and 2 to create a Nine-Patch unit, which should measure 4¼" square unfinished. Press the seams toward the top and bottom rows.

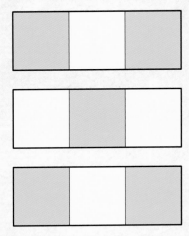

4. Draw a diagonal line once from corner to corner on the wrong side of both 5" cream print squares.

5. With right sides together, layer a marked 5" cream print square on top of a 5" red paisley square. Sew a ¼" seam on both sides of the line, then cut apart on the drawn line. Press the seam toward the red paisley triangle. Repeat this step for the other cream print and red paisley squares to make a total of four half-square triangle units.

6. Draw a diagonal line once from corner to corner on the wrong side of two half-square triangle units from the previous step.

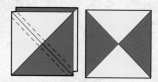

7. With right sides together, layer a marked half-square triangle unit on top of an unmarked half-square triangle unit, being careful to position the cream print triangles opposite of each other. Sew a ¼" seam on both sides of the line, then cut apart on the drawn line. Trim the star-point units to 4¼" square unfinished. Repeat with the other half-square triangle units to create a total of four star-point units.

8. Referring to the following block assembly diagram, sew together the Nine-Patch unit, the four units from the previous step, and the four 4¼" cream print squares to complete the block. The block should measure 11¾" square unfinished.

BLOCK ASSEMBLY DIAGRAM

❧ SAMPLER BLOCK BORDER FRAMES

Due to differences in the block sizes, we have added a red frame around each block to compensate for variations while spotlighting each block to full effect.

FOR BLOCK FRAMES, CUT:

* 16—1½" strips the width of fabric from red print

SEWING INSTRUCTIONS

1. Measure a sampler block and cut two 1½"-wide red print strips to match that measurement. Referring to the following diagram, sew a strip to each side of the block. Press the seams to the red print frame.

2. Measure the width of the unit from step 1 and cut two 1½"-wide red print strips to match that measurement. Referring to the previous diagram, sew a strip to the top and bottom of the unit from the previous step. Press the seams toward the red print frame.

3. Trim the block to measure 12½" square unfinished.

4. Repeat steps 1-3 for all 12 sampler blocks.

POINSETTIA BLOCK

FOR BLOCK BACKGROUNDS, CUT:

* ✳ 20—2½" x 4½" rectangles from cream print
* ✳ 20—2½" x 2½" squares from cream print
* ✳ 40—4½" x 6" rectangles from cream print
* ✳ 40—2½" x 3" rectangles from cream print

FOR GREEN LEAVES, CUT:

* ✳ 20—3" x 5" rectangles from green print
* ✳ 20—2" x 3" rectangles from green print

FOR POINSETTIA LEAVES, CUT:

* ✳ 10—2⅞" x 2⅞" squares from light red tone-on-tone
* ✳ 10—3¼" x 3¼" squares from light red tone-on-tone. Cut squares in half once diagonally to make 20 triangles
* ✳ 10—2⅞" x 2⅞" squares from dark red tone-on-tone
* ✳ 10—3¼" x 3¼" squares from dark red tone-on-tone. Cut squares in half once diagonally to make 20 triangles

SEWING INSTRUCTIONS

1. Draw a diagonal line once from corner to corner on the wrong side of the 2⅞" light red tone-on-tone squares.

2. With right sides together, layer a marked 2⅞" light red tone-on-tone square on top of a 2⅞" dark red tone-on-tone square. Sew a ¼" seam on both sides of the line, then cut apart on the drawn line. Press the seam toward the dark red tone-on-tone triangle. Trim the half-square triangle units to measure 2½" square unfinished. Repeat this step for the other light red tone-on-tone and dark red tone-on-tone squares to make a total of 20 half-square triangle units.

3. Referring to the following diagram for placement, sew together four half-square triangle units. The resulting unit should measure 4½" square unfinished. Repeat this step to make a total of five of these units. Press the seams toward the dark red tone-on-tone triangles.

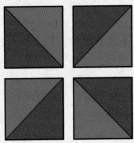

4. Using the 40—2½" x 3" cream print rectangles and 20—2½" x 3" green print rectangles, paper-piece 20 Small Leaf units, using the pattern on page 67. You will need to make a total of 20 of these units.

5. Referring to the following diagram, sew a Small Leaf unit to a 2½" cream print square. Press the seam toward the cream print square. Repeat to make 10 of these units.

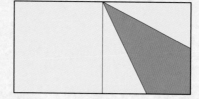

6. Referring to the following diagram, sew a reverse unit of the one shown in step 5. Repeat to make 10 of these units.

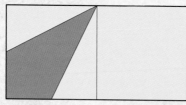

7. Referring to the following diagram, sew a 2½" x 4½" cream print rectangle to a Small Leaf unit from the previous step. Note the placement of the leaf changes according to its position. Press the seam toward the cream print rectangle. The resulting unit should measure 4½" square unfinished. You will need to make five units for each station as shown in the following diagram, for a total of 20 units.

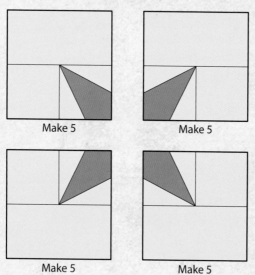

8. Using the 40—4½" x 6" cream print rectangles, 20—3" x 5" green print rectangles, 20 dark red triangles cut from the 3¼" dark red tone-on-tone squares, and 20 light red tone-on-tone triangles cut from the 3¼" light red tone-on-tone squares, paper-piece 20 Large Leaf units, using the pattern on page 67.

9. Referring to the following block assembly diagram, sew together four Small Leaf units, four Large Leaf units, and the unit from step 3 to complete one Poinsettia block. Press the seams toward the Large Leaf units. The block should measure 12½" unfinished. Repeat this step to make a total of five Poinsettia blocks.

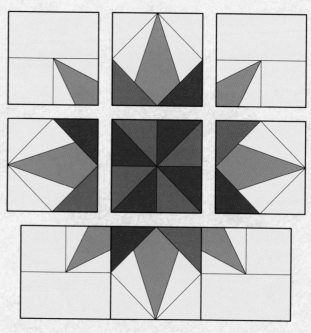

BLOCK ASSEMBLY DIAGRAM

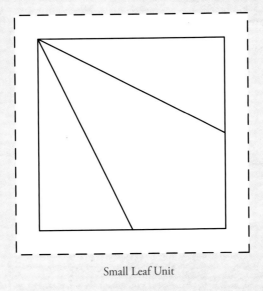

Small Leaf Unit

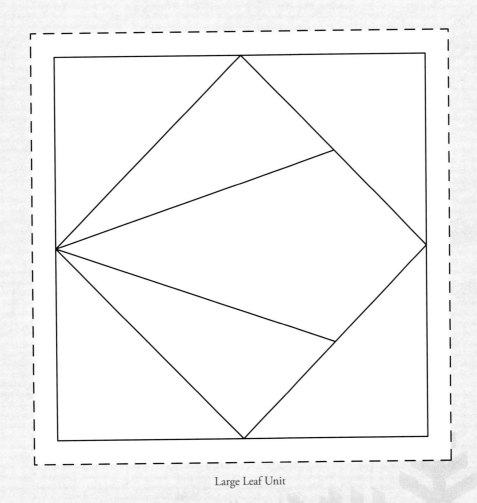

Large Leaf Unit

❧ Central Medallion Red Nine-Patch Blocks ❧

FOR RED NINE-PATCH UNITS, CUT:

* ✳ 2—2½" x 21" strips from red print
* ✳ 1—2½" x 11" strip from red print
* ✳ 1—2½" x 21" strip from cream print
* ✳ 2—2½" x 11" strips from cream print

FOR BLOCK BACKGROUNDS, CUT:

* ✳ 4—6½" x 6½" squares from cream print
* ✳ 4—6½" x 12½" rectangles from cream print

SEWING INSTRUCTIONS

1. Sew a 2½" x 21" red print strip to each side of a 2½" x 21" cream print strip. Press the seams toward the red print strips. Then cut the unit into eight 2½"-wide segments.

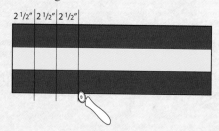

2. Sew a 2½" x 11" cream print strip to each side of a 2½" x 11" red print strip. Press the seams toward the red print strip. Then cut the strip into four 2½"-wide segments.

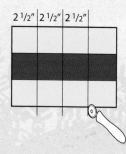

3. Sew together the three rows from steps 1 and 2 to create four Nine-Patch units, which should measure 6½" square unfinished. Press the seams toward the top and bottom rows.

4. Sew a 6½" cream print square to a red print Nine-Patch unit. Press the seam toward the cream print square. Repeat to make a total of four of these units.

5. Sew a 6½" x 12½" cream print rectangle to the bottom of the Nine-Patch unit from the previous step. Press the seam to the cream print rectangle. The resulting block should measure 12½" square unfinished. Repeat to make a total of four of these blocks.

GREEN NINE·PATCH
SETTING TRIANGLES

FOR SETTING TRIANGLES, CUT:

* 5—2½" strips the width of fabric from green print
* 4—2½" strips the width of fabric from cream print
* 12—7" x 7" squares from cream print. Then cut squares once diagonally from corner to corner, yielding two triangles

1. Sew a 2½ x width of fabric green print strip to each side of a 2½" x width of fabric cream print strip. Press the seams toward the green print strips. Repeat with two more green print strips and one more cream print strip. Then cut the units into 24—2½"-wide segments.

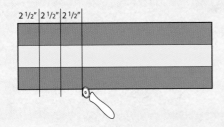

2. Sew a 2½" x width of fabric cream print strip to each side of a 2½" x width of fabric green print strip. Press the seams toward the green print. Then cut strips into 12—2½"-wide segments.

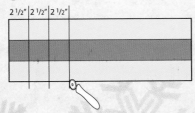

3. Sew together the rows from steps 1 and 2 to create a Nine-Patch unit, which should measure 6½" square unfinished. Press the seams toward the top and bottom rows. Repeat to make a total of 12 Nine-Patch units.

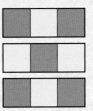

4. Referring to the following diagram, sew a cream print triangle cut from the 7" square to two adjacent sides of each green Nine-Patch unit. Press the seams toward the cream print triangles. Repeat to make a total of 12 of these units.

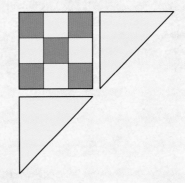

❦ Finishing the Quilt ❦

CUTTING INSTRUCTIONS

FOR SETTING SQUARES, CUT:
* 4—12½" x 12½" cream print squares

FOR CORNER TRIANGLES, CUT:
* 2—9⅜" x 9⅜" cream print squares. Then cut squares once diagonally from corner to corner, yielding two triangles

FOR INNER BORDER, CUT:
* 8—3½" strips the width of fabric from green print

FOR OUTER BORDER, CUT:
* 4—7" x 90" strips from red print

FOR BINDING, CUT:
* 9—2½" strips the width of fabric from red print

SEWING INSTRUCTIONS

QUILT CENTER
1. Referring to the quilt assembly diagram on page 71, sew the 12 sampler blocks, five Poinsettia blocks, four red Nine-Patch blocks, and 12 green Nine-Patch setting triangles into diagonal rows.

2. Join the rows from the previous step to complete the quilt center.

3. Sew the four corner triangles cut from the 9⅜" cream print square to the corners of the quilt center.

INNER BORDER
1. Sew together two 3½" x width of fabric green print strips. Repeat to create a total of four of these strips.

2. Measure your quilt top from top to bottom through the center and cut two green print border strips to match that measurement. Referring to the assembly diagram, sew the two strips to the opposite sides of the quilt top. Press the seams toward the green print border.

3. Measure your quilt top from side to side through the center and cut two green print border strips to match that measurement. Referring to the assembly diagram, sew the two strips to the top and bottom of the quilt top. Press the seams toward the green print border.

OUTER BORDER
1. Measure your quilt top from top to bottom through the center and cut two red print strips to match that measurement. Referring to the assembly diagram, sew the two strips to the opposite sides of the quilt top. Press the seams toward the red print border.

2. Measure your quilt top from side to side through the center and cut two red print strips to match that measurement. Referring to the assembly diagram, sew the two strips to the top and bottom of the quilt top. Press the seams toward the red print border.

3. Sandwich the quilt top, batting, and backing. Quilt as desired, then bind.

QUILT ASSEMBLY DIAGRAM

PROJECTS OF CHRISTMAS PAST

MEMORIES JOURNAL

MADE BY BETSEY LANGFORD AND EMILY CROSS

FINISHED SIZE: 11" X 16"

*R*ecord the memories of your Christmases past in this lovely companion journal. Designed to fit the common composition notebook, the cover can be customized with your favorite fabric. This versatile project also makes a handy daily organizer throughout the year.

MATERIAL REQUIREMENTS

JOURNAL COVER:
* ½ yard blue floral

JOURNAL LINING:
* ½ yard tan check

JOURNAL POCKETS AND EMBROIDERY BACKGROUND:
* ¼ yard or fat quarter tan solid
* ¼ yard or fat quarter tan print

9¾" x 7½" composition notebook
1½ yards fusible interfacing
DMC cream (739) embroidery floss

CUTTING INSTRUCTIONS

FOR JOURNAL COVER, CUT:
* 1—13" x 31" rectangle from blue floral
* 1—10¾" x 29" rectangle from fusible interfacing

FOR JOURNAL LINING, CUT:
* 1—13" x 31" rectangle from tan check
* 1—10¾" x 29" rectangle from fusible interfacing

FOR POCKETS, CUT:
* 1—7½" x 13" rectangle from tan solid
* 1—7½" x 6½" rectangle from fusible interfacing
* 1—7½" x 9" rectangle from tan print
* 1—4½" x 7½" rectangle from fusible interfacing

FOR EMBROIDERY BACKGROUND, CUT:

SEWING INSTRUCTIONS

1. Fuse the 10¾" x 29" interfacing to the wrong side of the 13" x 31" blue floral rectangle. Trim the blue floral rectangle to measure 11¾" x 30", centering the interfacing. This will leave the ½" seam allowances free of interfacing.

2. Fuse the 10¾" x 29" interfacing to the wrong side of the 13" x 31" tan check rectangle. Trim the tan check rectangle to measure 11¾" x 30", centering the interfacing. This will leave the ½" seam allowances free of interfacing.

3. With right sides together, layer the fused blue floral rectangle and the fused tan check rectangle. Using a ½" seam allowance, sew around the edges of the rectangle, leaving a 6" opening at the bottom center for turning it right side out.

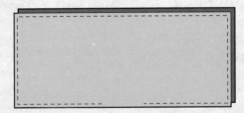

4. Trim the corners and turn the rectangle right side out.

5. Neatly turn the edges of the rectangle's opening in and press the cover.

6. With a pencil, trace the "Memories" pattern below onto the 9" tan solid square.

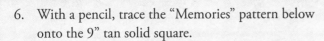

7. Using a backstitch, stitch the word "Memories" on the 9" tan solid square.

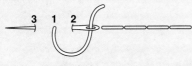

Backstitch

8. Centering the stitched embroidery, trim the tan solid square to 4½" x 6½". Fold the edges to the wrong side and press, leaving a 3½" x 5½" rectangle.

9. To position the stitched embroidery piece on the journal cover, measure one inch from the journal cover's center and topstitch it in place. Add any other desired embellishments.

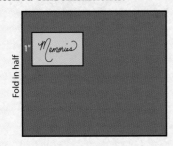

10. Fuse the 6½" x 7½" interfacing to the bottom half of the 7½" x 13" tan solid rectangle.

Interfacing

11. Fuse the 4½" x 7½" interfacing to the bottom half of the 7½" x 9" tan print rectangle. With wrong sides together, fold it in half and press lightly.

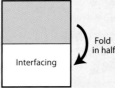

Interfacing

Fold in half

12. Lay the folded tan print rectangle on top of the right side of the 7½" x 13" fused tan solid rectangle on the fused end. Pin together at the sides.

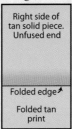

Right side of tan solid piece. Unfused end

Folded edge↗

Folded tan print

13. Sew a pencil pocket 1½" from the left edge. Then sew another pocket 1" from the first pocket, and another 1" from the previous one.

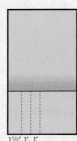

1½" 1" 1"

14. With right sides together, fold the non-interfaced side of the 7½" x 13" tan solid rectangle over the folded tan print pocket.

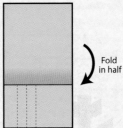

Fold in half

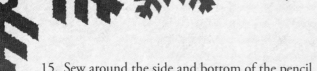

15. Sew around the side and bottom of the pencil pocket, leaving an opening on the right side.

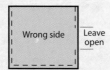

16. Trim the corners and turn the pencil pocket right side out. Turn the opening edges in neatly and press to complete the pocket unit.

17. Pin the pencil pocket unit to the front cover at the bottom right corner. Then topstitch the end edges of both ends of the cover.

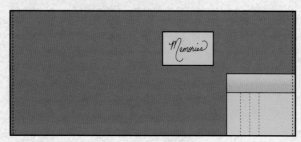

18. Turn the cover over so the tan check side is facing up. Fold the end with the pocket over so the pocket is at the folded edge. This will be the front inside flap. Pin the edges to hold the flap in place while leaving enough room to insert the composition notebook.

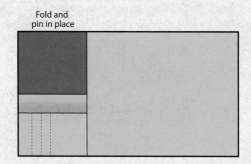

19. Slip the notebook into the front cover.

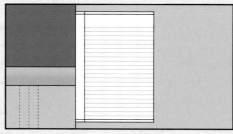

20. Bring the back cover over the back of the notebook. Pin in place.

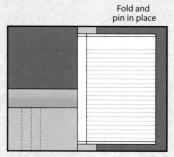

21. Close the notebook inside the cover to ensure it fits properly and that the cover is not so tight that it pulls the notebook open.

22. Remove the notebook, and starting with the journal's upper right-hand corner, topstitch the two sides down.

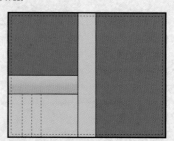

23. To insert the notebook into the cover, open it so wide that the front and back nearly touch. Then slide the front and back into the cover openings.

OHIO PATCH PICTURE

MADE BY CAROLYN NIXON

FINISHED BLOCK SIZE: 11" X 11"

Quilts aren't just for snuggling up in. They also make a striking statement on the wall. This variation on the Ohio Star block makes a stunning centerpiece when paired with a fitting frame.

MATERIAL REQUIREMENTS

OHIO PATCH BLOCK:
* ⅛ yard from cream print
* ⅛ yard from white print
* ⅛ yard from blue print
* ⅛ yard from dark blue print

BORDER:
* ⅛ yard from dark blue print

BACKING:
* 14" x 14" square muslin
* Square frame with a 14" x 14"-wide opening

CUTTING INSTRUCTIONS

FOR OHIO PATCH BLOCK, CUT:
* 4—4¼" x 4¼" squares cream print
* 1—5" x 5" square cream print
* 1—5" x 5" square white print
* 4—1¾" x 1¾" squares white print
* 2—5" x 5" squares dark blue print
* 5—1¾" x 1¾" squares blue print

FOR BORDER, CUT:
* 2—2½" x 11¾" strips from dark blue print
* 2—2½" x 15¾" strips from dark blue print

SEWING INSTRUCTIONS

1. Referring to the Ohio Patch block assembly instructions on pages 61-62, make an Ohio Patch block.

2. Trim the block to 11¾" square.

3. Referring to the assembly diagram below, sew the 2—2½" x 11¾" dark print strips to the sides of the Ohio Patch block. Then press the seams toward the border.

4. Referring to the assembly diagram, sew the 2—2½" x 15¾" dark blue print strips to the top and bottom of the Ohio Patch block. Then press the seams toward the border.

5. Sandwich block top, batting, and backing. Quilt as desired, then mount the block in a 14" frame, using the extra border material to stretch it.

PATCH PILLOW

MADE BY CAROLYN NIXON

FINISHED PILLOW: 16" X 16" • FINISHED BLOCK SIZE: 11" X 11"

Since we first started designing quilts, we have been enchanted with basket blocks. You can easily craft the feature quilt's basket block into a comfy pillow. Then simply choose the perfect nook in which to display your finished piece.

FABRIC REQUIREMENTS

Basket Patch block:
* ¼ yard cream print
* ⅛ yard tan print
* ⅛ yard blue print
* ⅛ yard dark blue print

Inner border:
* ⅛ yard blue print

Outer border:
* ¼ yard dark blue print

Pillow back:
* ¾ yard fabric of your choice

16" pillow form

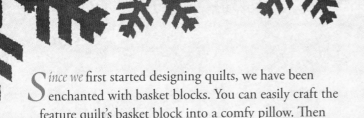

To make the smaller 14" x 14" pillow pictured in the photo on page 82, simply add a single 1¾"-wide border to the block and cut the backing fabric rectangles 15" x 20".

CUTTING INSTRUCTIONS

For Basket Patch block, cut:
* 1—5½" x 5½" square from cream print. Then cut square once diagonally from corner to corner, yielding two triangles. You will use only one triangle
* 2—2⅜" x 9" rectangles from cream print

* 1—4⅝" x 4⅝" square from cream print. Then cut square once diagonally from corner to corner, yielding two triangles. You will use only one triangle
* 2 Template As on page 34 from cream print (cut one reverse)
* 1 Template B on page 34 from cream print
* 2 Template Cs on page 34 from blue print (cut one reverse)
* 1 Template D on page 34 from blue print
* 1—2¾" x 2¾" square from blue print. Then cut square once diagonally from corner to corner, yielding two triangles
* 2—1⅞" x 3¾" rectangles from blue print
* 1—1⅞" x 1⅞" square from blue print
* 1—1⅞" x 3¾" rectangle from tan print
* 2—1⅞" x 1⅞" squares from tan print
* 1—3¾" x 3¾" square from dark blue print. Then cut square once diagonally from corner to corner, yielding 2 triangles. You will use only one triangle
* 1—7⅛" x 7⅛" square from dark blue print. Then cut square twice diagonally from corner to corner, yielding four triangles. You will only use two of these triangles

For inner border, cut:
* 2—1½" x 11½" strips from blue print
* 2—1½" x 13½" strips from blue print

For outer border, cut:
* 2—2¼" x 13½" strips from dark blue print
* 2—2¼" x 17" strips from dark blue print

For pillow backing, cut:
* 2—17" x 24" rectangles from fabric of your choice

SEWING INSTRUCTIONS

Basket Patch block and border
1. Referring to the Basket Patch block assembly instructions on pages 31-33, make a Basket Patch block.

2. Trim the block to 11½" square.

3. Referring to the diagram below, sew the 2—1½" x 11½" blue print strips and 2—1½" x 13½" blue print strips to the Basket Patch block. Press the seams toward the blue print border.

4. Referring to the diagram below, sew the 2—2¼" x 13½" dark blue print strips and 2—2¼" x 17" dark blue print strips to the pillow top. Press the seams toward the dark blue print border.

PILLOW BACK

1. With wrong sides together, fold each of the backing fabric rectangles in half.

2. Referring to the following diagram, overlap the folded end of the two backing fabric rectangles to create a 17" square. Then pin the pieces together to stabilize them.

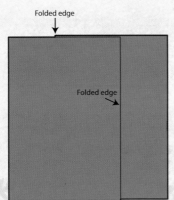

Folded edge

Folded edge

3. Flip the back over so the pins are on the outside. With right sides together, place the pillow front on the pillow back. Pin in place.

4. Using a ½" seam allowance, sew around the perimeter of the pillow.

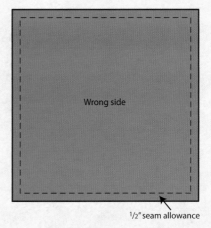

Wrong side

½" seam allowance

5. Trim the pillow corners, turn the pillow right side out, then press.

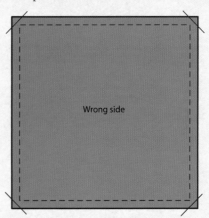

Wrong side

6. Insert the pillow form into the pillow through the overlap in the back.

SNOWFLAKE DANCE EMBROIDERY

STITCHED BY EMILY CROSS

FINISHED SIZE: 4½" X 4½"

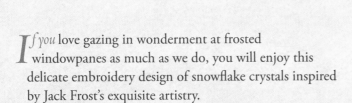

If you love gazing in wonderment at frosted windowpanes as much as we do, you will enjoy this delicate embroidery design of snowflake crystals inspired by Jack Frost's exquisite artistry.

FABRIC REQUIREMENTS

EMBROIDERY BACKGROUND:

* ❄ 12" square aged muslin

DMC white (B5200) embroidery floss

SEWING INSTRUCTIONS

1. Using an erasable marking pencil, lightly trace the design below onto the muslin square.

2. Backstitch the design below with three strands of white embroidery floss.

Backstitch

3. For the dots in the design below, use French knots.

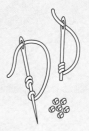

French Knot

4. Frame the stitchery as desired.

STAR PATCH TABLE RUNNER

MACHINE PIECED BY CAROLYN NIXON

QUILTED BY CAROLYN NIXON

FINISHED RUNNER: 14" X 39" • FINISHED BLOCK SIZE: 9" X 9"

Create a lovely holiday tabletop masterpiece using our Nine-Patch project as your canvas. We opted for the traditional yuletide color palette of red and green, but you can easily switch out the colors with ones that suit your particular fancy.

FABRIC REQUIREMENTS

BLOCK BACKGROUNDS:
* ⅛ yard gold print

STAR POINTS:
* ⅝ yard red print

NINE-PATCH UNITS:
* ⅛ yard cream homespun
* ⅛ yard green print

SASHING, BORDER, AND BINDING:
* ⅝ yard red print

BACKING:
* ½ yard fabric of your choice

CUTTING INSTRUCTIONS

FOR NINE-PATCH UNITS, CUT:
* 15—2" x 2" squares from green print
* 12—2" x 2" squares from cream homespun

FOR STAR POINTS, CUT:
* 12—3⅛" x 3⅛" squares from red print

FOR BLOCK BACKGROUNDS, CUT:
* 3—5¾" x 5¾" squares from gold print
* 12—2¾" x 2¾" squares from gold print

FOR SASHING AND BORDER, CUT:
* 4—3½" x 9½" rectangles from red print
* 2—3½" x 39½" strips from red print

FOR BINDING, CUT:
* 3— 2½" strips the width of fabric

SEWING INSTRUCTIONS

STAR PATCH BLOCKS

1. Referring to the Star Patch block assembly instructions on pages 48-49, make a Star Patch block. Repeat to make a total of three of these blocks.

2. Trim the three blocks from step 1 to 9½" square.

FINISHING THE RUNNER

1. Referring to the assembly diagram below, join the three Star Patch blocks and 4—3½" x 9½" red print rectangles in a row. Press the seams toward the red prints.

2. Referring to the assembly diagram, sew the 2—3½" x 39½" red print strips to the top and bottom of the unit from Step 1. Press the seams toward the border.

3. Sandwich the table runner top, batting, and backing. Quilt as desired, then bind.

SUPER STAR THROW

MACHINE PIECED BY CAROLYN NIXON

MACHINE QUILTED BY LIZ KERR

FINISHED THROW: 60" X 60"   •   FINISHED BLOCK SIZE: 12" X 12"

*W*e love designing quick and easy projects. This comfy throw is a cinch to whip up. Select seasonal fabrics for holiday flair or pick a color palette to complement your home décor throughout the year.

FABRIC REQUIREMENTS

STAR:

* 1½ yards cream print
* ¾ yard red floral
* ¾ yard green print

BORDER:

* 1¾ yards red floral

BINDING:

* ½ yard red floral

BACKING:

* 5 yards fabric of your choice

CUTTING INSTRUCTIONS

FOR STAR, CUT:

* 4—12½" x 12½" squares from cream print
* 4—13" x 13" squares from cream print
* 4—13" x 13" squares from green print
* 4—13" x 13" squares from red floral

FOR BORDER, CUT:

* 4—6½" strips the length of fabric from red floral

FOR BINDING, CUT:

* 15—2½" strips the width of fabric from red floral

SEWING INSTRUCTIONS

1. Draw a diagonal line on the back of the 13" cream print squares and two of the 13" red floral squares.

2. With right sides together, layer a 13" cream print square on top of an unmarked 13" red floral square. Sew a ¼" seam on both sides of the drawn line. Then cut apart on the drawn line and press open to yield two half-square triangle units. Repeat to make a total of four cream/red half-square triangle units.

3. Repeat step 2 with the remaining 13" cream print squares and two of the 13" green print squares to make a total of four cream/green half-square triangle units.

4. Repeat step 2 with the marked 13" red floral squares and two of the 13" green print squares to make a total of four red/green half-square triangle units.

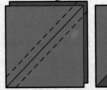

5. Trim all half-square triangle units to 12½" square, using the diagonal seam as the center guide.

91

6. Referring to the assembly diagram below, assemble the 12 half-square triangle units from steps 2-5 and the 4—12½" cream print squares into four rows. Then join the rows to create the block.

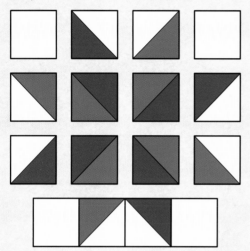

7. Measure the throw from top to bottom through the center, then cut two of the 6½"-wide red floral strips to match that measurement. Then sew these two strips to the sides of the throw.

8. Measure the throw from side to side through the center, then cut two of the 6½"-wide red floral strips to match this measurement. Then sew these two strips to the top and bottom of the throw.

9. Sandwich the throw top, batting, and backing. Quilt, then bind.

One Piece at a Time by Kansas City Star Books – 1999

More Kansas City Star Quilts by Kansas City Star Books – 2000

Outside the Box: Hexagon Patterns from The Kansas City Star by Edie McGinnis – 2001

Prairie Flower: A Year on the Plains by Barbara Brackman – 2001

The Sister Blocks by Edie McGinnis – 2001

Kansas City Quiltmakers by Doug Worgul – 2001

O' Glory: Americana Quilt Blocks from The Kansas City Star by Edie McGinnis – 2001

Hearts and Flowers: Hand Appliqué from Start to Finish by Kathy Delaney – 2002

Roads and Curves Ahead: A Trip Through Time with Classic Kansas City Star *Quilt Blocks* by Edie McGinnis – 2002

Celebration of American Life: Appliqué Patterns Honoring a Nation and Its People by Barb Adams and Alma Allen – 2002

Women of Grace & Charm: A Quilting Tribute to the Women Who Served in World War II by Barb Adams and Alma Allen – 2003

A Heartland Album: More Techniques in Hand Appliqué by Kathy Delaney – 2003

Quilting a Poem: Designs Inspired by America's Poets by Frances Kite and Deb Rowden – 2003

Carolyn's Paper Pieced Garden: Patterns for Miniature and Full-Sized Quilts by Carolyn Cullinan McCormick – 2003

Friendships in Bloom: Round Robin Quilts by Marjorie Nelson and Rebecca Nelson-Zerfas – 2003

Baskets of Treasures: Designs Inspired by Life Along the River by Edie McGinnis – 2003

Heart & Home: Unique American Women and the Houses that Inspire by Kathy Schmitz – 2003

Women of Design: Quilts in the Newspaper by Barbara Brackman – 2004

The Basics: An Easy Guide to Beginning Quiltmaking by Kathy Delaney – 2004

Four Block Quilts: Echoes of History, Pieced Boldly & Appliquéd Freely by Terry Clothier Thompson – 2004

No Boundaries: Bringing Your Fabric Over the Edge by Edie McGinnis – 2004

Horn of Plenty for a New Century by Kathy Delaney – 2004

Quilting the Garden by Barb Adams and Alma Allen – 2004

Stars All Around Us: Quilts and Projects Inspired by a Beloved Symbol by Cherie Ralston – 2005

Quilters' Stories: Collecting History in the Heart of America by Deb Rowden – 2005

Libertyville: Where Liberty Dwells, There is My Country by Terry Clothier Thompson – 2005

Sparkling Jewels, Pearls of Wisdom by Edie McGinnis – 2005

Grapefruit Juice and Sugar: Bold Quilts Inspired by Grandmother's Legacy by Jenifer Dick – 2005

Home Sweet Home by Barb Adams and Alma Allen – 2005

Patterns of History: The Challenge Winners by Kathy Delaney – 2005

My Quilt Stories by Debra Rowden – 2005

Quilts in Red and Green and the Women Who Made Them by Nancy Hornback and Terry Clothier Thompson – 2006

Hard Times, Splendid Quilts: A 1930s Celebration, Paper Piecing from The Kansas City Star by Carolyn Cullinan McCormick – 2006

Art Nouveau Quilts for the 21st Century by Bea Oglesby – 2006

Designer Quilts: Great Projects from Moda's Best Fabric Artists – 2006

Birds of a Feather by Barb Adams and Alma Allen – 2006

Feedsacks! Beautiful Quilts from Humble Beginnings by Edie McGinnis – 2006

Kansas Spirit: Historical Quilt Blocks and the Saga of the Sunflower State by Jeanne Poore – 2006

Bold Improvisation: Searching for African-American Quilts – The Heffley Collection by Scott Heffley – 2007

The Soulful Art of African-American Quilts: Nineteen Bold, Improvisational Projects by Sonie Ruffin – 2007

Alphabet Quilts: Letters for All Ages by Bea Oglesby – 2007

Beyond the Basics: A Potpourri of Quiltmaking Techniques by Kathy Delaney – 2007

Golden's Journal: 20 Sampler Blocks Honoring Prairie Farm Life by Christina DeArmond, Eula Lang and Kaye Spitzli – 2007

Borderland in Butternut and Blue: A Sampler Quilt to Recall the Civil War Along the Kansas/Missouri Border by Barbara Brackman – 2007

Come to the Fair: Quilts that Celebrate State Fair Traditions by Edie McGinnis – 2007

Cotton and Wool: Miss Jump's Farewell by Linda Brannock – 2007

You're Invited! Quilts and Homes to Inspire by Barb Adams and Alma Allen of Blackbird Designs – 2007

Portable Patchwork: Who Says You Can't Take it With You? by Donna Thomas – 2008

Quilts for Rosie: Paper Piecing Patterns from the '40s by Carolyn Cullinan McCormick – 2008

Fruit Salad: Appliqué Designs for Delicious Quilts by Bea Oglesby – 2008

Red, Green and Beyond by Nancy Hornback and Terry Clothier Thompson – 2008

A Dusty Garden Grows by Terry Clothier Thompson – 2008

We Gather Together: A Harvest of Quilts by Jan Patek – 2008

With These Hands: 19th Century-Inspired Primitive Projects for Your Home by Maggie Bonanomi – 2008

As the Cold Wind Blows by Barb Adams and Alma Allen of Blackbird Designs – 2008

Caring for Your Quilts: Textile Conservation, Repair and Storage by Hallye Bone – 2008

The Circuit Rider's Quilt: An Album Quilt Honoring a Beloved Minister by Jenifer Dick – 2008

Embroidered Quilts: From Hands and Hearts by Christina DeArmond, Eula Lang and Kaye Spitzli – 2008

Reminiscing: A Whimsicals Collection by Terri Degenkolb – 2008

Scraps and Shirttails: Reuse, Re-purpose and Recycle! The Art of Green Quilting by Bonnie Hunter – 2008

Flora Botanica: Quilts from the Spencer Museum of Art by Barbara Brackman – 2009

Making Memories: Simple Quilts from Cherished Clothing by Deb Rowden – 2009

Pots de Fleurs: A Garden of Applique Techniques by Kathy Delaney – 2009

Wedding Ring, Pickle Dish and More: Paper Piecing Curves by Carolyn McCormick – 2009

The Graceful Garden: A Jacobean Fantasy Quilt by Denise Sheehan – 2009

My Stars: Patterns from The Kansas City Star, Volume I – 2009

Opening Day: 14 Quilts Celebrating the Life and Times of Negro Leagues Baseball by Sonie Ruffin – 2009

St. Louis Stars: Nine Unique Quilts that Spark by Toby Lischko – 2009

Whimsyland: Be Cre8ive with Lizzie B by Liz & Beth Hawkins – 2009

Cradle to Cradle by Barbara Jones of Quilt Soup – 2009

Pick of the Seasons: Quilts to Inspire You Through the Year by Tammy Johnson and Avis Shirer of Joined at the Hip – 2009

Across the Pond: Projects Inspired by Quilts of the British Isles by Bettina Havig – 2009

Artful Bras: Hooters, Melons and Boobs, Oh My! A Quilt Guild's Fight Against Breast Cancer by the Quilters of South Carolina - 2009

Flags of the American Revolution by Jan Patek – 2009

Get Your Stitch on Route 66: Quilts from the Mother Road by Christina DeArmond, Eula Lang and Kaye Spitzli from Of One Mind – 2009

Gone to Texas: Quilts from a Pioneer Woman's Journals by Betsy Chutchian – 2009

Juniper and Mistletoe: A Forest of Applique by Karla Menaugh and Barbara Brackman - 2009

My Stars II: Patterns from The Kansas City Star, Volume II – 2009

Nature's Offerings: Primitive Projects Inspired by the Four Seasons by Maggie Bonanomi – 2009

Quilts of the Golden West: Mining the History of the Gold and Silver Rush by Cindy Brick – 2009

Women of Influence: 12 Leaders of the Suffrage Movement by Sarah Maxwell and Dolores Smith of Homestead Hearth– 2009

Adventures with Leaders and Enders: Make More Quilts in Less Time! by Bonnie Hunter – 2010

A Bird in Hand: Folk Art Projects Inspired by Our Feathered Friends by Renee Plains – 2010

Feedsack Secrets: Fashion from Hard Times by Gloria Nixon – 2010

Greetings from Tucsadelphia: Travel-Inspired Projects from Lizzie B Cre8ive by Liz & Beth Hawkins – 2010

The Big Book of Bobbins: Fun, Quilty Cartoons by Julia Icenogle – 2010

Country Inn by Barb Adams and Alma Allen of Blackbird Designs – 2010

My Stars III: Patterns from The Kansas City Star, Volume III – 2010

Piecing the Past: Vintage Quilts Recreated by Kansas Troubles by Lynne Hagmeier – 2010

Stitched Together: Fresh Projects and Ideas for Group Quilting by Jill Finley – 2010

A Case for Adventures by Katie Kerr – 2010

A Little Porch Time: Quilts with a Touch of Southern Hospitality by Lynda Hall – 2010

Circles: Floral Applique in the Round by Bea Oglesby – 2010

Comfort Zone: More Primitive Projects for You and Your Home by Maggie Bonanomi – 2010

Leaving Baltimore: A Prairie Album Quilt by Christina DeArmond, Eula Lang and Kaye Spitzli from Of One Mind – 2010

Like Mother, Like Daughter: Two Generations of Quilts by Karen Witt and Erin Witt – 2010

Sew Into Sports: Quilts for the Fans in Your Life by Barbara Brackman – 2010

Under the Stars by Cherie Ralston – 2010

A Path to the Civil War: Aurelia's Journey Quilt by Sarah Maxwell and Dolores Smith of Homestead Hearth – 2010

Across the Wide Missouri: A Quilt Reflecting Life on the Frontier by Edie McGinnis and Jan Patek – 2010

Cottage Charm: Cozy Quilts and Cross Stitch Projects by Dawn Heese – 2010

My Stars IV: Patterns from The Kansas City Star, Volume IV – 2010

Roaring Through the 20s: Paper Pieced Quilts from the Flapper Era by Carolyn Cullinan McCormick – 2010

PROJECT BOOKS

Fan Quilt Memories by Jeanne Poore – 2000

Santa's Parade of Nursery Rhymes by Jeanne Poore – 2001

As the Crow Flies by Edie McGinnis – 2007

Sweet Inspirations by Pam Manning – 2007

Quilts Through the Camera's Eye by Terry Clothier Thompson – 2007

Louisa May Alcott: Quilts of Her Life, Her Work, Her Heart by Terry Clothier Thompson – 2008

The Lincoln Museum Quilt: A Reproduction for Abe's Frontier Cabin by Barbara Brackman and Deb Rowden – 2008

Dinosaurs - Stomp, Chomp and Roar by Pam Manning – 2008

Carrie Hall's Sampler: Favorite Blocks from a Classic Pattern Collection by Barbara Brackman – 2008

Just Desserts: Quick Quilts Using Pre-cut Fabrics by Edie McGinnis – 2009

Christmas at Home: Quilts for Your Holiday Traditions by Christina DeArmond, Eula Lang and Kaye Spitzli from Of One Mind - 2009

Geese in the Rose Garden by Dawn Heese – 2009

Winter Trees by Jane Kennedy – 2009

Ruby Red Dots: Fanciful Circle-Inspired Designs by Sheri M. Howard – 2009

Backyard Blooms: A Month by Month Garden Sampler by Barbara Jones of QuiltSoup – 2010

Not Your Grandmother's Quilt: An Applique Twist on Traditional Pieced Blocks by Sheri M. Howard – 2010

A Second Helping of Desserts: *More Sweet Quilts Using Pre-cut Fabric* by Edie McGinnis – 2010

Café au Lait: Paper Piece a Rocky Road to Kansas by Edie McGinnis – 2010

Border Garden by Lynne Hagmeier – 2010

From the Bedroom to the Barnyard: A 9-Block Sampler Honoring Barn Quilts – 2010

Picnic Park by Barbara Jones of QuiltSoup – 2010

HOT OFF THE PRESS PATTERNS

Cabin in the Stars by Jan Patek – 2009

Arts & Crafts Sunflower by Barbara Brackman – 2009

Birthday Cake by Barbara Brackman – 2009

Strawberry Thief by Barbara Brackman – 2009

French Wrens by Dawn Heese - 2010

QUEEN BEES MYSTERIES

Murders on Elderberry Road by Sally Goldenbaum – 2003

A Murder of Taste by Sally Goldenbaum – 2004

Murder on a Starry Night by Sally Goldenbaum – 2005

Dog-Gone Murder by Marnette Falley – 2008

DVD PROJECTS

The Kansas City Stars: A Quilting Legacy – 2008

HOMEMADE LOVE

Homemade love surrounds me
In a kaleidoscope of colors;
A Log Cabin and Grandmother's Flower Garden,
A Wedding Ring and Grandmother's Fan,
A festival of colors and patterns
Made by loving hands.

    In the mirror of my mind
    Reflections appear –

        A scrap bag,
        Discarded dresses,
        Daddy's old shirts,
        Calico, paisley, and stripes.

        Mama's hands,
        With a cardboard pattern
        And silver scissors,
        Cuttin' out the pieces,
        Stackin' 'em in a pile.

        Her nimble fingers
        Fly across the pieces
        Of multicolored fabric
        Makin' tiny little stitches.

The reflections fade
From the mirror of my mind . . .
But I can still see Mama's hands
In the soft blanket of patterns and colors
Surrounding me with homemade love.

        —Carolyn Brown Nixon